PRAISE FOR *HIRING SECRETS OF THE NFL*

"I thoroughly enjoyed this book, especially the warnings about using the wrong metrics and the importance of approaching hiring systematically."

—Usha Chaudhary, Executive Vice President and Chief Financial Officer, United Way of America

"Really fun—I think you have a hit on your hands. The parallels between the NFL draft and corporate hiring work really well."

—Mark Coronna, Chief Marketing Officer, Wolters Kluwer Financial Services

"The ultimate playbook for today's leaders and managers, to help them identify, hire, and retain 'game-changing' talent who can help win the big game versus bringing more 'position players' on board who can't or won't take your organization's performance to the next level."

—Tony Abena, Senior Vice President, Thomson Corporation

"Using professional football as a metaphor, paints a vivid picture of how to build corporate champions."

—Thomas J. Valerius, Vice President, Recruitment Services, UnitedHealth Group

"A novel and enjoyable analysis of how aggressive process improvement is the foundation of winning dynasties, in football and in business."

—Eric Educate, Chief Marketing Officer, Fair Isaac Corporation

HIRING SECRETS of the NFL

HIRING
SECRETS
of the NFL

HOW YOUR COMPANY
CAN SELECT TALENT
LIKE A CHAMPION

ISAAC CHEIFETZ

Davies-Black Publishing
Mountain View, California

Published by Davies-Black Publishing, a division of CPP, Inc., 1055 Joaquin Road, 2nd Floor, Mountain View, CA 94043; 800-624-1765.

Special discounts on bulk quantities of Davies-Black books are available to corporations, professional associations, and other organizations. For details, contact the Director of Marketing and Sales at Davies-Black Publishing: 650-691-9123; fax 650-623-9271.

NFL is a registered trademark of the National Football League. Davies-Black and its colophon are registered trademarks of CPP, Inc.

Visit the Davies-Black Publishing Web site at www.daviesblack.com.

Printed in the United States of America.

11 10 09 08 07   10 9 8 7 6 5 4 3 2 1

Library of Congress Cataloging-in-Publication Data
Cheifetz, Isaac
  Hiring secrets of the NFL : how your company can select talent like a
  champion / Isaac Cheifetz.—1st ed.
    p. cm.
  Includes bibliographical references and index.
  ISBN: 978-0-89106-219-6 (hardcover)
  1. Employee selection. I. Title.
  HF5549.5.S38H572 2007
  658.3'112—dc22

                                                              2007016040

FIRST EDITION
First printing 2007

To my friend Bill, for hanging in there to see this book published

CONTENTS

KICKOFF

Every year, football fans dream that their team will draft the next Lawrence Taylor or Alan Page. Some years they are rewarded with stars, some with stiffs. The NFL® drafting process is at least as sophisticated as the corporate hiring process these days, with psychological assessments, IQ tests, breakdowns of college performance, and examinations of physical ability.

How can football teams and companies maximize the chances of selecting future stars? This book is an attempt to define the rules of success for talent selection in the NFL and the corporate ranks.

The origins of this book are interesting. It did not require much research or interviewing, but sprung nearly fully formed based on my work and interests over the course of my career. I am an executive recruiter, a headhunter, with twenty years of experience consulting to advanced technology businesses on executive search, organizational design, and strategy.

As for sports, I was a rabid fan in high school and college, but as the years went on I found myself following sports less. Hockey, baseball, and college basketball each fell to the wayside. Even my NBA obsession dimmed, as the NBA draft came to resemble a high school prom. Yet my fascination with the NFL draft actually grew. Between recruiting calls, I found myself surfing Web sites dedicated to NFL mock drafts and prospect evaluations, first in the months before the draft and, after a couple of seasons, all year long.

Occasionally I would admonish myself for wasting time. Why not choose to analyze balance sheets in my spare time, like Warren Buffett? I hardly watched NFL games on TV anymore, yet was fascinated by the interplay between predraft projection, draft selection, and career performance.

One day it hit me: trying to predict the performance of NFL prospects feels familiar because it has so much in common with my day job, helping companies hire executive talent. I specialize in searches for executives who can help companies in rapidly changing industries, particularly those attempting to leverage information technology for strategic advantage. The business model and/or position are often new, and predicting success is even more difficult than usual.

Football has much in common with the corporate world. Success in both results from complex plans aggressively and precisely executed. In both, it is challenging to select personnel with the appropriate balance of raw ability and accomplishment and difficult even to define conclusively what experience is critical to success in the position. Yet mistakes are costly in both football and corporate human capital.

The corporate talent selection process resembles that of football more than that of baseball or basketball. As described in *Moneyball,* Peter Lewis's best seller on the Oakland A's, a baseball player's statistics are easier to define, lending themselves to analysis more than the human talent selection and assessment process in business, or football. The NBA is a poor analog to the corporate world, because in the NBA superstars are indispensable and rare. The concept prevalent in football and business that no one person is indispensable doesn't apply as much in the NBA. Teams do win championships without a Shaq or a Michael Jordan, but they are the exception.

Of course, there are significant differences between the NFL and business. A business career can easily span twenty-five to forty years, while NFL careers are far shorter. Even stars rarely play much more than twelve years, and careers are routinely ended by injury. Indeed, using football as a metaphor for business organizations has limitations, given the violence inherent in the game, and the ruthlessness with which personnel decisions are made.

To sum it up, this book is about how to build champions, in football and in business. The first eight chapters each focus on a critical success factor for selecting talent in the NFL and its application in business. The final chapter outlines a model for applying these principles to your business to improve the efficiency, speed, and results of corporate hiring.

ACKNOWLEDGMENTS

I would like to thank the following individuals:

- Writers who particularly influenced me in the writing of this book:
  - Michael Holley, author of *Patriot Reign: Bill Belichick, the Coaches, and the Players Who Built a Champion*
  - Pete Williams, author of *The Draft: A Year Inside the NFL's Search for Talent*
  - Professor Boris Groysberg of Harvard Business School, particularly for his *Harvard Business Review* articles "Are Leaders Portable?" and "The Risky Business of Hiring Stars"
  - George Plimpton, for setting a lyrical standard in the writing of NFL books with *Paper Lion* and *Mad Ducks and Bears*
  - Peter Drucker, for inventing the study of management and writing about it so well, for so long
  - George Orwell, whose nonfiction informs everything I think and write

- John Oslund, business research editor of the *Minneapolis Star Tribune*, for first giving me the opportunity to write a monthly column, one of which is the basis of this book

- Scott Edelstein, my agent and editorial consultant, who went beyond the call of duty in helping me write and market this book

- Connie Kallback, formerly senior acquisitions editor at Davies-Black Publishing, who made writing and editing my first book a joy

- The production, marketing, and sales teams at Davies-Black for their professionalism and energy

- The many friends and colleagues who encouraged me to continue on this path, particularly the members of the Sushi Club, aka "Isaac's Brain Truss" (no, that's not a misspelling)

- My dear friends Bill and Mira Akins, whose friendship and support the past fifteen years have enriched my life in so many ways

- And most especially, my wife, Kelli, and stepdaughter, Chloe, for their patience and support while I wrote this book at all hours, as well as for their general forbearance and love

ABOUT THE AUTHOR

Isaac Cheifetz has nearly twenty years' experience consulting on executive search, organizational design, and strategy. Since founding Open Technologies in 1992, he's been helping companies hire senior executives who have demonstrated their ability to leverage technologies to build profitable businesses. He has consulted to early-stage business-to-business e-commerce ventures on strategy, organizational design, and raising investor financing. He has served as a CEO coach for many early-stage companies.

Isaac received a bachelor's degree in history from Yeshiva University in 1981. An interest in the time and motion studies of Frederick Taylor led him to graduate studies in organizational psychology at Columbia University, where he received a master of arts degree in 1983. Graduate school loans drove him into the deep end of the pool as an executive recruiter in 1986. Working with the firms building the technologies that became the foundation of the Internet revolution, he developed a deep set of practical skills around hiring and retaining key executives.

CHAPTER 1

DRAFTING BY POSITION

Determine the Essence of the Job

When I was playing, I never worried about a guy that ran a 4.4 forty, if I watched the film and saw that he had 5.2 hands.
—Herm Edwards, head coach, Kansas City Chiefs[1]

In the NFL and in business, a position will have a variety of attributes considered important for success. But for most roles, there are a very small number of skills that are critical—their absence will dictate failure.

 ## SECRET 1
Discover the "True Must" of the Position

The "true *must* of the position," as Pete Prisco of CBS Sports-Line.com calls it, is the critical success factor of the position, without which achievement is impossible. Lacking the true

TABLE 1 *"True Musts" vs. Merely Desirable Traits in Football*

Football Position	True Musts	Desirable Trait
Receiver	Great hands, disciplined route runner	Great speed
Quarterback	Calm under pressure, awareness, leadership	Great arm
Offensive lineman	Tenacious, strong, smart	Superior size and athleticism

must for a role, elite ability is useless. Table 1 describes the true must for several football positions.

Table 2 shows that in business, too, there is a true must for nearly every role, without which success is unlikely, regardless of the individual's ability. Note that key intangibles such as discipline and motivation are not addressed here, on the assumption that all roles in football and business require them.

TABLE 2 *"True Musts" vs. Merely Desirable Traits in Business*

Business Role	True Musts	Desirable Trait
Sales rainmaker	Tenacity, professionalism	Charisma and organization
Start-up CEO	Ability to analyze the market, identify opportunities, and design and execute strategies appropriate to the company	Vision. A new venture benefits from a leader who can paint a vision of where the company is going and how it will transform its industry; being a successful leader requires just enough creativity to win, yet not so much as to get lost.
CIO	Balancing technical and business realities; fulfilling commitments	Technical vision; but a brilliant architect who is a weak manager of projects or people will leave a trail of unfinished products and political turmoil.

SECRET 2
Hire for the Needs of the Future, Not the Past

Consider a software firm whose growth has stalled and which hires a president who was wildly successful during the boom era of the 1990s. Then remember that a successful executive in that era was rewarded for trying to hit home runs—to grow a large company and to have a successful IPO.

Software has since become a mature, rather than a growth, industry, and standards for companies going public are more rigorous in today's Sarbanes-Oxley environment. A software firm is more likely to be successful attacking niche vertical markets, rather than attempting broad rapid growth. Acquisition by a larger firm is a more likely long-term goal than an IPO.

To successfully grow a software firm under these new conditions, a successful IPO might be less relevant than a track record of efficiently building solutions targeted to specific industries and constructing successful channel relationships.

Carly Fiorina at HP

Few executives in recent history have had the charisma of Carly Fiorina, CEO of Hewlett-Packard from 1999 to 2005. She was strategically creative and highly articulate. Her ability to motivate employees and customers was considered critical to HP's turnaround. She had established a track record as a successful sales executive during the 1980s and '90s, the golden age of the computer industry. But Fiorina had no track record of large-scale, long-term operational excellence, nor was she a visionary.

Unfortunately, by 1999 the PC industry had become unprofitable for everyone but Dell, the FedEx of the PC industry. HP would have been better off pursuing a niche strategy, investing in its profitable businesses, such as printing and imaging, and retaining the profitable instrument division, rather than spinning it off as an IPO into Agilent. HP should have gradually stepped away from the low-margin PC market, as IBM had done, rather than spending $24 billion to acquire Compaq and doubling up its bet on PCs.

Carly Fiorina was dismissed by HP's board of directors in February 2005. Hewlett-Packard's CEO as of this writing, Mark Hurd, is less of a star than Carly Fiorina, but his successful track record in making NCR Teradata a profitable niche vendor explains his current success at HP.

 ## SECRET 3
Don't Ignore Key Secondary Attributes

Sometimes a person with strengths in a key attribute can mimic competence in other critical, yet secondary, attributes. A brilliant specialist or salesperson being groomed for a top job may lack "emotional intelligence," or EQ, the concept popularized by Daniel Goleman in the 1990s that includes factors such as self-awareness, altruism, personal motivation, and empathy. This part of his makeup is so underdeveloped that over time he is held to a lower standard than his peers, like a dog that has reduced his frequency of in-house "accidents" from regular to occasional.

Similarly, when this talented individual evolves his interpersonal skills from crude to adequate, he may be judged ready to lead. But he has probably only learned to mimic these skills, to apply them by rote. When challenged by new circumstances under crisis conditions, his veneer of leadership skills will quickly wear down and he will be forced to fall back on his lifetime of stunted interpersonal skills. Rude competence can be an effective management style, as long as the leader is consistent and tough-minded. Consider the disparate cases, and outcomes, of three brilliant, undiplomatic leaders: Jack Welch, Rudy Giuliani, and Larry Summers.

Jack Welch

Jack Welch is now considered the greatest CEO of recent times. These days, we take for granted the ruthless culture he created at GE, in the context of all the money made for investors, the jobs created, and the industries resuscitated. But Welch was reviled as "Neutron Jack" (after the cold war nuclear weapon designed to kill people and leave buildings intact) when he laid off 25 percent of GE's workforce in the 1980s. Welch insisted he was doing the kindest thing by giving managers clear feedback as to their market value sooner, rather than later.

It is important to note that GE was a successful company when Welch became its CEO in 1981. He had the support of the board of directors for revitalizing the company, and he was competent, consistent, honest, and ruthless on the path to ultimate success.

Rudy Giuliani

Rudy Giuliani's calm leadership as mayor of New York City on and after 9/11 made him a hero. In the previous seven years, he was an unusually effective change agent, but he was anything but universally popular.

When Giuliani became mayor in 1994, New York had long been considered ungovernable. Giuliani had previously achieved some fame as the prosecuting district attorney who broke the power of the New York Mafia. As mayor, he brusquely confronted established interest groups. More critically, he instructed the NYPD to enforce aggressive zero-tolerance policies for offenses such as subway turnstile jumping and trespassing, based on the "broken window" theory that tolerating petty crimes creates a culture conducive to serious crimes. He also applied advanced software decision support systems to crime fighting.

During Giuliani's time in office the crime rate went down dramatically, and his techniques were adopted in cities across the country. But his aggressive policing and disdain for social welfare constituencies created a furor in traditionally liberal New York. Giuliani was lambasted by opponents as a fascist and a racist, no doubt hurtful to a man whose domestic political and social philosophies were consistently liberal. Giuliani knew he would be judged by his results and did not care for the dubious support of rigid ideologues or cynical hustlers.

Larry Summers

In 2006, Larry Summers resigned his position as president of Harvard University. In five years, he had gone from being considered the next great American university president to a besieged, controversial figure, accused by detractors of racial and sexual insensitivity.

Summers, a brilliant economist, joined the Clinton administration in 1993 as undersecretary of the treasury for international affairs. In this role he served as brilliant sidekick to Treasury Secretary Robert Rubin, a polished former Wall Street executive. Rubin attempted to smooth Summers's rough edges, particularly his intellectual arrogance. Summers took the challenge seriously and improved his diplomatic skills sufficiently to be named to replace Rubin as secretary when Rubin resigned in 1999.

Summers served ably as treasury secretary and was appointed president of Harvard in 2001 with the mandate of "shaking things up."[2] He attempted to improve the quality of undergraduate education at Harvard, of which its world-class faculty had become neglectful in recent years.

However, in his attempt to shake things up, Summers chose to criticize the lack of focus of an African American studies professor and pondered aloud whether there might be a biological basis to the underrepresentation of women professors in science and engineering. His reasoning was based in esoteric statistical analysis of research that showed that though men and women test equally in IQ, men may have a wider range of intelligence between the smartest and dumbest, while women may be closer in intelligence on average to each other. (Think of this as the Albert Einstein–Curly Howard continuum of male intelligence.)

The Harvard faculty, already threatened by Summers's questioning of their time spent researching versus teaching, used these controversies to attack Summers as "insensitive," if not reactionary. Summers is actually an idealistic liberal by any standards other than those of the fevered swamps of a politically correct campus. In both episodes Summers quickly apologized for his comments. But his apologies encouraged his critics, and, after several stormy years, he resigned to become a professor at Harvard once again.

Why wasn't Summers effective as president of Harvard after serving in sensitive leadership roles at the highest levels of government? Summers is a classic example of a talented specialist who gained just enough polish to lead a stable organization, but whose lack of sophistication as a leader was exposed under the pressure of trying to change it.

To Summers, diplomacy was primarily learning not to be abusive to others. He never had to learn how to deal with others being abusive to him. He had grown in emotional intelligence in the context of government and national politics, shielded by a charismatic, lightning-rod president, Bill Clinton, during the longest economic boom in U.S. history.

Though he had spent most of his life in academia (both his parents were professors, and two of his uncles are Nobel Prize–winning economists), he had no previous academic administrative experience. One of the youngest full professors in Harvard's history at age twenty-eight, he had consistently been rewarded for being brilliantly disruptive intellectually in several fields of economics. He was a notoriously idealistic and abrasive truth seeker.

At Treasury, Summers was rigorously disciplined in his public utterances, in consideration of their impact on global financial markets. Once back in academia, he reverted to form as a naïve idealist. It probably did not occur to him that being right, and somewhat more polite, was not enough to succeed. He was therefore helpless in the face of the passive-aggressive attacks of pampered faculty.

What might Summers have done differently in order to succeed as president of Harvard? A more sophisticated leader would have been more calculating, even manipulative, in choosing his battles. He would have had few illusions about the community of coddled professors he was attempting to transform. He would have anticipated their inevitable personal attacks on him and have had a much thicker skin in the face of their insults, like Rudy Giuliani. He would have anticipated the impact of controversial actions or statements, made them with intent, and not made tepid apologies afterward. He would realize that, as university president, it was no longer beneficial to try to be the "smartest guy in the room"—that was now irrelevant and counterproductive.

Had Summers confronted the true requirements of the job ahead of time, he most likely would have not taken it.

 # SECRET 4
Choose a "4-3" or a "3-4" Sales Model

In the NFL, the two primary defensive line configurations are the "4-3," with four defensive linemen and three linebackers, and the "3-4," with three linemen and four linebackers.

A 4-3 or a 3-4 Defense

In a 4-3 defense, the linemen are the primary pass rushers. They are known as "one-gap" linemen, each responsible for a single lane between the opposing offensive linemen. They aggressively attack that gap in pursuit of the other team's quarterback or running back.

In a 3-4 defense, the linemen have "two-gap" responsibility. As a result, they must be bigger (3-4 linemen rarely weigh less than 300 pounds) and are primarily responsible for controlling the opponent's offensive line, freeing the linebackers to rush the passer and make the tackles.

Smart NFL teams who play a 3-4 are careful to draft linemen who fit their defensive scheme. Many linemen can play in either defensive system, but most do best in one or the other. Aside from the additional size the 3-4 requires, many college

linemen are accustomed instinctively to penetrating the opponent's backfield, rather than playing the more systemic role of
controlling the line of scrimmage.

A 4-3 or 3-4 Sales Model

How does a 4-3 model differ from a 3-4 model in business?
A 4-3 sales model is a classic sales-driven organization, where
the sales reps are responsible for penetrating new accounts. It
requires salespeople to be aggressive and compensates them
accordingly.

A 3-4 sales model is driven by account management, rather
than new sales. The account reps still have revenue responsibility, but because they are primarily farming within existing
accounts, they have more of a consultative role across the customer life cycle and often have broader industry expertise.

Deciding whether you are a 4-3 or 3-4 sales organization is
critical for determining how you hire and compensate your
salespeople. A 3-4 sales model often has world-class sales reps,
but they have different responsibilities and are compensated
differently.

For example, IBM is a 3-4 sales organization, despite being a
highly respected training ground for IT sales. The account executives generally sell to existing customers and are part of a team,
with a customer service mentality. They are well compensated,
but they know they could make more if they moved to a firm
that emphasizes a sole contributor sales model.

Oracle, in contrast, is a 4-3 sales organization, where sales
reps are hunters. They are highly compensated but ruthlessly
judged on their revenue production (somewhat like an NFL
coach, come to think of it).

Table 3 describes the varying responsibilities and requirements of a 4-3 versus a 3-4—in the NFL and in corporate sales.

TABLE 3 *The 4-3 vs. the 3-4*

Football Structure	Lineman Responsibilities	Lineman Requirements
4-3 defense	Relentlessly attack the quarterback	Speed, aggressiveness, athletic ability
3-4 defense	Control line of scrimmage, allowing linebackers to attack the quarterback	Massive size, strength, strategic awareness, patience
Business Structure	**Salesperson Responsibilities**	**Salesperson Requirements**
4-3 sales model	Increase sales by penetrating new accounts	Aggressiveness, charisma, high energy
3-4 sales model	Increase sales by improving account management	Industry expertise, consultative skills, patience

SECRET 5
Keep It Simple

The best indicator of future performance is past performance—"betting on form," as the horse-racing expression goes. Challenging this statistical rule of nature is OK, as long you don't invest too much on these bets.

If your obsession drives you nonetheless to continue on this path, you may be the next great innovator in your profession: the next Bill Belichick, coach of the New England Patriots; the next Ross Perot, founder of EDS and the computer outsourcing industry; or the next Fred Smith, founder of Federal Express and next-day delivery. But be aware that most revolutionary businesses are radically innovative in one—and only one—aspect, whether it's technology for Apple or logistics for Dell.

I often caution entrepreneurs who are breaking the mold in some critical aspect of their business that they ought to be energetically but unimaginatively competent in their hiring practices. The risk to the organization of innovating on more than one front at a time is nearly insurmountable.

HIGHLIGHTS

In the NFL and in business, a position will have a variety of attributes considered important for success. But for most roles, only a very small number of skills are critical—their absence will dictate failure.

SECRET 1
Discover the "true must" of the position

SECRET 2
Hire for the needs of the future, not the past

SECRET 3
Don't ignore key secondary attributes

SECRET 4
Choose a "4-3" or a "3-4" sales model

SECRET 5
Keep it simple

CHAPTER 2

"SPORTSMANLIKE" CONDUCT

Value Character

One of the terms I've learned to be sensitive to is risk and reward. Now when I hear it in a character context, I don't want those players on the team.

—Arthur Blank, owner, Atlanta Falcons, and founder of Home Depot[3]

Organizations that tolerate superstars who are personally productive but organizationally disruptive rarely attain world-class performance.

It is unusual for a dysfunctional NFL superstar to win a championship. The famous exception is Lawrence Taylor, "L.T.," the New York Giants linebacker (1981–93) who revolutionized his position and led the Giants to two Super Bowl wins while combating a full-blown addiction to crack cocaine. But Taylor was a uniquely talented gamechanger, powerfully driven to win, and surrounded by other great defenders who were emotionally stable. He is the exception that proves the rule.

SECRET 6
Eliminate Teamwreckers

In his 1990 book *Million Dollar Habits,* Robert Ringer devotes a chapter to "The Drain People Elimination Habit." He describes "drain people" as those "who drain you of time, energy, peace of mind, relaxation, comfort and/or money."[4]

A wide range of these drain people, or "teamwreckers" as I call them, populate the corporate world. Let's examine four categories of teamwreckers: the *morally challenged,* the *narcissist,* the *walking wounded,* and the *situational teamwrecker.*

The Morally Challenged

Morally challenged individuals are likely to act on their worst instincts at some point. If in a leadership role, they can corrupt a culture or deform it. Even if they miraculously don't influence others, can you watch them every moment of the day? How much energy will that take? Where could you better use that energy to grow your business?

The human condition being what it is, many people have the potential for morally dubious actions. An organization led by an amoral leader may succeed for a time, but in the long term it will be seriously damaged when challenged by unforeseen events. It's possible to establish an ethical business culture and demand that ethical and legal standards be upheld; it is much more difficult to reform an unethical adult.

The Narcissist

Narcissists' consuming goal is to look great. Winning is the best way to accomplish this, whether in sports or business, which often makes them appear to be valuable. But if narcissists can look great in defeat, they will be satisfied in that case, too.

The Walking Wounded

The walking wounded inhabit a different psychological landscape from that of people who are emotionally whole. Their internal strife drives them to create and then perpetuate conflict where none exists. Here are the three varieties of walking wounded, from least harmful to most harmful: the *crab*, the *backstabber*, and the *scorpion*.

The Crab. In a pail full of crabs, some will reflexively pull back anyone who attempts to better himself by climbing out of the pail. Every organization has powerful political undercurrents, but the "crab" culture is paralyzed by politics. A high-performing organization will swiftly cast out crabs, but a critical mass of crabs can create a culture in which losing is considered preferable to taking chances. Crabs are losers, or at the very least have become habituated to losing.

Transforming a long-term losing culture may unfortunately require a "scorched earth" policy of dismissing many players, leaving the "turnaround" coach who rids the team of its losing mentality without enough talent left to win. A case in point is the revival of the New York Giants in the early 1980s. When Ray Perkins became head coach in 1979, the Giants had not been to the playoffs in eighteen years. Perkins, a "Bear" Bryant protégé at Alabama, was hired to change the Giants' losing culture—

which he did, by ruthlessly driving the team to work harder and play smarter. Yet the Giants were never more than respectable under Perkins, and it was not until his assistant Bill Parcells took over in 1984 that the Giants began to excel.

There is little evidence that corporations with grossly dysfunctional cultures can be changed gradually. In the real world, a better vision for the future and tighter organizational discipline may not be enough. A certain amount of tension, even fear, may be necessary to separate those willing to commit to the new culture from those who lack the motivation or ability to abandon their losing mind-set.

The Backstabber. Backstabbers are competent, but they put significant energy into subverting their peers. In football, the organizational structure and culture constrains overt backstabbing, with the gap between players and coaches resembling that of union workers and management.

In a corporate management setting, where politics are ubiquitous, a skilled backstabber can cut with the dexterity of a surgeon. A company can make its culture less hospitable to backstabbers, even if it can't realistically screen them all out in the hiring process. Putting results above all else will provide less cover to individuals who compete politically. Backstabbers then will tend to migrate to companies whose cultures are more hospitable to their machinations.

The Scorpion. Scorpions are talented, hardworking individuals who are driven to destroy their work environment, and ultimately their own careers, due to inner emotional turmoil.

The Scorpion's Logic—"It's in my nature to sting."

A scorpion was wandering along the bank of the river, wondering how to get to the other side. Suddenly he saw a fox. He asked the fox to take him across the river. The fox said, "No. If I do that, you'll sting me and I'll drown." The scorpion assured him, "If I did that, we'd both drown."

The fox thought about it and finally agreed. So the scorpion climbed up on his back and the fox began to swim. But halfway across the river, the scorpion stung him. As the poison filled his veins, the fox turned to the scorpion and said, "Why did you do that? Now you'll drown too."

The scorpion shrugged, and did a little jig on the drowning fox's back. "I couldn't help it," said the scorpion. "It's in my nature to sting."

—Traditional folktale

Terrell Owens is the ultimate scorpion, a cartoonlike archetype highlighting the temptations and perils of bringing talented teamwreckers into an organization. "T.O." is a big, fast, powerful, hardworking receiver, but he is deeply self-destructive. Yet for all his touchdowns, Owens has never played for a winning team beyond the first round of the playoffs.

Granted, his San Francisco teams were mediocre, and he did have several great games in the playoffs for them. But his attempts at publicly degrading Jeff Garcia, the 49ers' undistinguished successor to star quarterback Steve Young, led a second-rate team to implode.

When Owens forced a trade to the Philadelphia Eagles in 2004, he joined a team on the verge of greatness, which had lost in the conference championships four years in a row. He put up gaudy numbers during the regular season but missed the first two playoff games due to injury, which the Eagles won without him. With great fanfare, he played injured in the Super Bowl, which the Eagles lost.

Owens, a fan favorite in the 2004 Super Bowl year, was reviled in 2005 for his obnoxious behavior. Few pointed out, however, that he had no obvious contribution to their getting further in the playoffs that year. The Eagles won during the regular system with him, as they had in previous years before his arrival. They won two playoff games to get to the Super Bowl while he was out due to injury, though his presence seemed to give confidence to the team.

The next season, Owens held out for a new contract and more money, taking his case public by again publicly attacking his team's quarterback, in this case superstar Donovan Mc-Nabb. His disruptive behavior cast a pall over the Eagles, who eventually suspended and then released him.

At most, Owens served as a psychological shot in the arm for a team with some self-doubt—a playoff placebo. The next year, he was bad medicine indeed, devastating the team emotionally. A fan favorite in the 2004 Super Bowl year, he was reviled in 2005 for his obnoxious behavior.

Owens has deeply rooted emotional reasons for his dysfunctional behavior. These reasons are murky to others but are critical to his self-image and self-expression, or he would not be so regular and decisive in acting them out, on one team after another.

Owens, as of the 2006–07 season a Dallas Cowboy, will likely torment fans in Dallas for another year or two before imploding. By then his extraordinary gifts will have eroded enough to reduce the temptation of owners and GMs to bring the ultimate teamwrecker onto their team.

The Situational Teamwrecker

The situational teamwrecker is a follower who will go along with the dominant culture, positive or negative. This person will act badly in a culture that is habituated to losing, but will be productive and loyal if transferred to a *stable* winning organization. An example of this is Corey Dillon, whose moodiness as a star running back on a terrible Cincinnati Bengals team disappeared once he was traded to the New England Patriots, where he helped them win another Super Bowl. But beware: In business or in football, situational teamwreckers love to portray themselves as victims of a dysfunctional environment. If the organization is not currently dysfunctional, they will rock the boat until it is—to prove their point.

Situational teamwreckers should be presumed guilty until proven innocent. Even if they are well intentioned, they are expressing themselves childishly and are not going to lead the organization from losing to winning. To succeed, they require an already stable organization.

 ## SECRET 7
Understand the Hidden Costs of Teamwreckers

Avoiding teamwreckers is more easily said than done. The temptation to keep them around springs from their incredible talent, especially since they are often driven and hardworking.

Companies are sometimes afraid to rein in disruptive stars. But a superachiever who demeans and manipulates his peers can disrupt the output of the entire department. Consider these two varieties of high-performing corporate disrupters: the *rainmaker* and the *IT guru*.

The Rainmaker

The temptation to tolerate star salespeople who abuse those around them is powerful. High-performing sales reps are often an odd combination of thick-skinned and emotionally sensitive, empathetic and manipulative. A sales culture often has a merrily obnoxious quality. And performance in sales is individually measured, like with a baseball hitter at the plate.

A wise sales manager once said: "Great sales reps either have really high or really low self-esteem. The 'highs' deal with rejection by assuming there is something wrong with you, not them. The 'lows' have such low self-esteem that they are numb to rejection."

Both sales types can be successful (and many stars have elements of both), but happy sales stars are the foundation of a much healthier sales organization. They are less likely to misuse the organizational influence derived from their revenue generation and suck energy from other functions and their peers in sales. They also serve as a positive role model for ambitious junior sales reps as to how to behave. The "problem children" of tomorrow will act out in any case, but many individuals will vary in their behavior, in sports or companies, based on the implicit rules of the organization.

Albert the Destroyer

Albert was bright, charismatic, ambitious, and the top salesperson in his division. He rose to be a manager, then a vice president. He was also a bully, whose ambition came in part from some psychic wound. It was not enough for him to succeed—he spent a sizable part of his time diminishing the reputation and self-esteem of his subordinates, his peers, and *their* subordinates.

For years, the company dealt with "Albert incidents" on an individual basis, treating them as a cost of doing business. His behavior often made the firm an unpleasant place to work, but he was the biggest moneymaker in the company, both as an individual contributor and as a sales manager.

Eventually, the management of the firm sent Albert packing, after belatedly concluding that the firm's success was based on organizational, not individual, output. No one person was as gifted or productive as Albert, but he was reducing the total output of dozens of sales reps by a significant proportion. The company successfully expanded nationally with a sales model that emphasized performance and alignment with product strategy over a "star rep" strategy. Albert started his own manufacturer's rep firm and was wildly successful.

The IT Guru

Software gurus earn their salaries. The complexity of software architecture is staggering—it is the design of an imaginary castle in the clouds, described in a foreign language. The variance between the production of a competent software programmer and a great one is monumental, not incremental.

Some of the best technologists are near-geniuses who spend their days inside that castle in the clouds. Some have trouble communicating well, and some, in the words of a *Dilbert* cartoon, have an emotional makeup that combines Dustin Hoffman's autistic character in *Rainman* with Sean Penn assaulting a photographer.

For years, software vendors tolerated brilliant but volatile geniuses due to their outsized impact. Sometimes, if these individuals were charismatic enough to be promoted, they created entire obnoxious organizations in their own image. Across the country in management information systems (MIS) environments, lesser lights imitated the disturbed guru model, whether or not they were truly indispensable. But as the size of software systems grew, software development increasingly became a collaborative endeavor and the dysfunctional savant had an increasingly negative impact.

In addition, the drive toward software standardization has decreased (for now) the value of solitary geniuses who build systems software without direct business application. For business applications, the IT guru model may actually be detrimental. In *Decline and Fall of the American Programmer,* Edward Yourdon, a pioneering software methodologist, forecast correctly that India would rise as a global center for software development, not just because of cost advantages, but because Indian software developers were more willing to discipline themselves to software process methodologies.[5] The "creative" self-image of many American software engineers, according to Yourdon, would become increasingly less relevant to the challenge of raising the maturity of software development as an engineering discipline.

Even the Open Source software movement, which gives talented developers the opportunity to contribute to major systems development projects, is inherently a collaborative effort, and it is in any case generally an uncompensated one.

There is, and will always be, a need for the isolated genius, the writer of algorithms, or the game designer. Just be sure he is producing like a mad genius, not just acting like one.

SECRET 8
Assess Arrogance and Disruption Relative to Function

In the NFL, certain positions tend to display more arrogance than others. The "skill" positions on offense seem to dominate, possibly because they score the touchdowns and are therefore most obvious to fans. Quarterbacks are less likely to be obnoxiously arrogant, as they are only effective if they possess strong leadership skills as well as a powerful arm.

But it is the wide receiver position where outlandish behavior is most tolerated, even expected. Why wide receivers? Being on the receiving end of the most spectacular plays feeds their ego (like salesmen), and their distance downfield from the bulk of the violence on the line gives them a distorted sense of the realities of the game (like software gurus).

Though teams routinely win Super Bowls with good—rather than great—wide receivers, mature superstar wide receivers are rare treasures. Interestingly, they are often good rather than great athletes who excel due to intangibles rather than athletic prowess. Marvin Harrison of the Indianapolis Colts is one. Another is Torry Holt of the St. Louis Rams, Super Bowl winners in 1999 powered by an overwhelming passing offense nicknamed "The Greatest Show on Turf." Holt contributed to winning both through offensive production and by not stressing out the team with egocentric demands for more catches. Unlike with Randy Moss when he was with Minnesota, there was never a "Torry Ratio" in St. Louis.

Consistently Excellent, Reserved Holt, Anti-T.O.

What makes St. Louis Rams receiver Torry Holt so good?
"He gets his catches because he's the best route runner in the league," Rams quarterback Marc Bulger said. "I've

never seen a guy who has more naturally gifted hands," Rams coach Scott Linehan said. "He makes every catch look so easy."

Both good reasons, but Holt provides the No. 1 reason. "I pride myself on my consistency," Holt said. "It's the same every year. Some guys it's hot, warm, and then cold. Or it's hot, lukewarm, cold and then hot again. For me, I like it to be about consistency. The other way makes no sense to me. . . ."

"He's not a self-promoter," Linehan said. "He's very secure. He doesn't need the spotlight. He doesn't need all the attention. But there is little doubt that he plays at the highest level in this league."

—*Pete Prisco, August 9, 2006, CBS SportsLine.com*

Successful business organizations, like winning teams, require emotional maturity from all employees, but the standards for various roles differ. Emotional balance and decorum should be benchmarked relative to the standards of high performers in their function, rather than well-balanced performers with average output.

Salespeople will be rambunctious; equity analysts will be arrogant. To some extent, these characteristics are inherent in the nature of those jobs and sometimes are what you pay them to project to the market. Moreover, high performers are by nature somewhat insecure and prone to acting out.

Certain roles, even entire industries, are more likely to attract individuals confident to the point of egotism. After a meeting between a software executive and an industry analyst, the executive observed pensively, "You know, he's not very arrogant for an analyst." Winning NFL teams seek high performers who are grown up by NFL standards, and successful corporations should hire executives who are well adjusted by the standard of fast-track executives. Both groups are substantially different from society's average.

In the corporate world, talented individuals in traditionally less glamorous occupations such as logistics or accounting may sometimes seem "too loud" compared to their peers. Their emotional makeup often makes them more appropriate for a sales role, which, combined with their specialist experience, can turn them into superstar salespeople. These are hidden treasures, potentially the leaders of tomorrow.

In my formative years as a headhunter, the three most successful recruiters in my firm were trained accountants, who after several years at accounting firms realized that they had resources of internal aggression that would not be satisfied in a role that lacked the thrill of the chase.

 ## SECRET 9
Don't Try to Fix a Teamwrecker

As a team executive famously said to the star of an abysmal team who was demanding more money, "We lost with you, we can lose without you." So if we have proven conclusively that an organization composed of teamwreckers won't win, why do NFL general managers and business executives continue to hire them? There are several reasons.

Optimism

Optimism can make an arrogant or naïve hiring team or firm believe that they will be able to manage the teamwrecker productively where others could not. When they discover that they are not able to, the relationship often develops a powerful co-dependent dynamic, in which, as psychologist Robert Subby has written, "a set of dysfunctional rules within a family or social system . . . interfere with healthy growth and make constructive change very difficult, if not impossible."[6]

Coaches are arrogant and unrealistic when they believe they can motivate underachievers where others have failed. They often become codependent with "coach killers," players whose potential tempts coaches to invest excessive time, resources, and energy on them but whose dysfunction leads to the team's underperforming and the coach's ultimate firing.

Insecurity

Sometimes the retention of teamwreckers indicates a lack of confidence. The GM knows that chemistry matters and has no illusions about his ability to change the player, but he is desperate to entertain the fans and does not think a dysfunctional talented player can make things worse. The Green Bay Packers' signing of wide receiver Koren Robinson in September 2006 after the Vikings waived him for his latest drunk-driving escapade may be viewed in this light.

This grasping at straws is a sign that not only are the current prospects of the team poor, but the longer-term plan is not well defined—or supported—by ownership. It also presumes that fans are stupid. In fact, fans prefer to root for overachievers rather than talented underachievers. A .500 team composed of ordinary talents who play hard and smart is a heartwarming morality play; a team of championship-caliber talent that wins just half its games is frustrating.

In the business world, a touch of emotional dysfunction often correlates positively with high achievement. A truly emotionally content person is more likely to find Zen-like satisfaction in the status quo than to fight to improve on it.

But if ankle-deep emotional dysfunction can spur athletes or executives to overachieve, knee-deep dysfunction will slow them down, waist-deep dysfunction will bring them to a standstill, and neck-deep dysfunction will likely pull their coaches and teammates, or managers and co-workers, down below the water's surface with them. Table 4 compares dysfunction and performance.

You can measure the value of a teamwrecker by the following formula:

$$\text{Value} = \text{Personal Output} \div \text{Negative Impact on Team Performance}$$

Talented people who are self-indulgent and resist dedicating their abilities to the organization's goal are like a cannon aimed into the fort rather than outside of it. You're better off taking your chances without them.

TABLE 4 *Valuing Teamwreckers: Dysfunction vs. Performance*

Level of Dysfunction	Level of Performance
Ankle deep	High performance, moderate maintenance
Knee deep	High performance, high maintenance
Waist deep	Low performance, high maintenance
Neck deep	Reduces organization's output; drowns those who try to save them

HIGHLIGHTS

Organizations that tolerate superstars who are personally productive but organizationally disruptive rarely attain world-class performance.

SECRET 6
Eliminate teamwreckers

SECRET 7
Understand the hidden costs of teamwreckers

SECRET 8
Assess arrogance and disruption relative to function

SECRET 9
Don't try to fix a teamwrecker

CHAPTER 3

OUT OF BOUNDS

Welcome Eccentrics

[I'd like to play] Robin Hood . . . I've always wanted to wear a pointed green hat with a long feather in it.
—**Alex Karras, former defensive tackle, Detroit Lions**[7]

The frustration of managing difficult personalities, in sports or business, often leads to fantasies of winning with a team of hard workers with above-average talent and being able to avoid quirky personalities altogether. The danger in this is achieving consistent mediocrity.

SECRET 10
Seek Talented Eccentrics

Knowledge workers who create, analyze, and synthesize information are central to today's global economy, and unusual creative ability is a powerful competitive advantage.

Eccentricity Defined

Eccentricity refers to unusual or odd behavior on the part of an individual. This behavior would typically be perceived as unusual or unnecessary, without being demonstrably maladaptive. . . . Eccentrics will sometimes find unconventional solutions to problems.

—*Wikipedia*

Great talents and high achievers often are eccentric people with outsized abilities, usually with outsized quirks and imperfections. They resemble a high-powered but badly wired sports car, like a 1970s Jaguar, whose electrical system was so unreliable detractors nicknamed it the Prince of Darkness.

Elite talent will usually beat ordinary talent if it can only stay on the racetrack. It is pointless for the Jag (or the Jag's supervisor) to envy the Toyota Camry for its reliability. The race car doesn't have to be as reliable as the family sedan; it will win races if it is more reliable than other race cars.

In the NFL, teamwreckers may not be worth the trouble, but talented nonconformists are. The Oakland Raiders won multiple Super Bowls by collecting talented oddballs with a deep desire to win, after they were discarded by other teams.

Two of the greatest defensive tackles in NFL history, Alex Karras and Warren Sapp, were deeply eccentric, brash, and antiauthoritarian, while leading dominating defenses. Andy Grove represents a counterpart to them in business.

Alex Karras

Karras was one of the dominant defensive players of the 1960s. He was a squat, powerful, and absurdly fast defensive tackle, nicknamed "The Mad Duck" for his devastating quarterback rushes. He was thoughtful, eloquent, and funny, with the timing of a stand-up comic, yet unapologetic about occasionally cheap-shotting opponents.

Karras was a disciplined player on the field but went out of his way to play the role of rebel in public, achieving off-field notoriety when he was suspended by NFL Commissioner Pete Rozelle for the 1964 season for gambling on football games (he spent the year moonlighting as a professional wrestler). Later, as an actor, he achieved fame for his role as Mongo in the Mel Brooks movie *Blazing Saddles,* in which he knocked out a horse with one punch.

Warren Sapp

A 6'2", 300-pound defensive tackle, Warren Sapp was an All-American at the University of Miami, with an unusual combination of power and speed. He was the top-rated defensive tackle in the 1995 draft, but a positive test for marijuana and a reputation for wildness gave him the label of a potential draft bust.

The Tampa Bay Buccaneers selected Sapp with the twelfth pick in the draft, based on extensive research that convinced them that he was in fact deeply dedicated to the game—and to winning. According to Pete Williams in *The Draft,* "Sapp, though a bit of a handful, was a true talent and a student of the game. He could talk at length about teams that thrived before he entered grade school, especially such dominating defenses as the Pittsburgh Steelers' 'Steel Curtain,' the Minnesota Vikings' 'Purple People Eaters,' or the 'Doomsday Defense' of the Dallas Cowboys."[8]

Sapp quickly became the anchor of the great Tampa Bay defense, which dominated the NFL for much of the next decade, and won the Super Bowl in 2003.

Andy Grove

Andy Grove is considered one of the great modern CEOs for his leadership of Intel Corporation in the 1980s and '90s. But for much of his career he was considered an eccentric by corporate standards. In a 1983 essay on Intel founder Robert Noyce, writer Tom Wolfe described how unusual the laid-back corporate culture at Intel seemed to East Coast businesspeople, and how Grove in particular dressed more like a disco dancer than Noyce's lieutenant responsible for Intel's operations.[9]

Political Dissident—A Job Only a Crazy Person Would Take?

Are eccentrics more likely to attempt and achieve unusually difficult goals? A sobering example is the Soviet Union's persecution of political dissidents in the 1970s through the abuse of psychiatry. Nonconformists who fought for freedom of speech and religion were routinely diagnosed as mentally ill by state psychiatrists and institutionalized. By the Soviet definition, anyone who challenged the "perfection of the workers paradise" was by definition neurotic, antisocial, and paranoid.

The Western psychiatric community was horrified by the Soviet abuses of medicine and independently analyzed the case studies of the institutionalized dissidents. To their surprise, they were often unable to definitively prove the diagnoses wrong.

Many dissidents, in turned out, were indeed neurotic and paranoid. This did not conflict with their courage and heroism. Wouldn't it help to be a little crazy to challenge the totalitarian Soviet state?

SECRET 11
Distinguish Eccentrics from Teamwreckers

It is critical not to confuse eccentricity with dysfunction. Unfortunately, both eccentrics and teamwreckers are often resistant to authority, insisting on marching to the beat of a different drummer. How can you tell them apart? Table 5 provides some clues.

TABLE 5 *Eccentrics vs. Teamwreckers*

Eccentrics	Teamwreckers
Eccentrics are deeply driven to help their team win, though they may define their "team" as their peers, rather than the formal organization.	Teamwreckers care about winning insofar as it benefits them, whether financially or egotistically.
Eccentrics are idealistic, often naïve. They tend to be deeply honorable and ethical. They are constantly shocked that the world is not a better place and that organizations do not do the right thing more often.	Teamwreckers are cynical and self-serving. If they seem naïve, it is because their ego is blocking their vision. They are constantly shocked that the world does not spoon-feed them all that they desire. They are prone to unethical behavior.
Eccentrics are ridiculed from a distance, but gain respect the more you know them. Their surface social awkwardness eventually pales against the light of their considerable inner qualities.	Teamwreckers often project an impressive image, but become less attractive the more you are exposed to them.
Eccentrics tend to be intrinsically motivated (à la management theorist Frederick Herzberg) and value the challenge of their work and the quality of the surrounding environment over financial rewards. They crave respect from their peers more than they do public recognition.	Teamwreckers are extrinsically motivated by financial rewards and formal recognition. For teamwreckers, in the words of Mick Jagger, "too much is never enough." They are deeply sensitive to, and suspicious of, being disrespected.

Eccentrics should be assessed relative to their function and industry. Creative jobs that reward concentrated abstract thinking will attract individuals who spent their formative years building intellectual rather than social skills.

SECRET 12
Recognize the Varieties of Eccentrics

Eccentrics don't seem as strange once you learn to recognize the key varieties of the breed. Here are several:

■ **The "oblivious eccentric."** This spaceman commutes daily from his home planet, yet puts in a full day with a craftsman's work ethic.

■ **The "free spirit eccentric."** He cares deeply about winning and his peers but is deeply resistant to top-down control, especially if it does not directly concern his work product. The late Pat Tillman was a good example of this. Tillman, the Arizona Cardinals safety who left the NFL in 2002 to enlist in the U.S. Army Rangers, died in combat in Afghanistan in 2004. His life was a series of iconoclastic choices and accomplishments: a hard-hitting football star who enjoyed meditating atop a light tower; an overachieving "coaches' dream" who refused to allow his college coaches to dictate his academic program or graduation schedule. Tillman's decision to turn down a multimillion-dollar contract to join the army was typical for a free spirit who was deeply committed to his team and, ultimately, his country.

■ **The "bored eccentric."** An eccentric whose energies are not well utilized, he may act out in an immature fashion.

- **The "obnoxious eccentric."** OK, eccentrics are really a pain. Truth is, sometimes you need them. If everyone on your team is well balanced, who will be the organization's source of creative destruction?

The following profiles serve to illustrate types of eccentrics in football and business.

Randy Moss

Wide receiver Randy Moss is on the bubble between being a teamwrecker and an eccentric, but he is ultimately an example of how a superstar can distort his team's strategy while underachieving on his true strategic potential.

Moss, like Terrell Owens, is a receiver with striking gifts. He is 6'4" with sprinter speed, the leaping ability of a basketball star, and amazingly soft hands. Uniquely among NFL receivers, these gifts have allowed him to catch almost any pass thrown in his direction (in the same way the NBA's Kareem Abdul-Jabbar could score using his height and skyhook whenever he wanted).

Moss does not have a history of major conflict with teammates and has been enormously productive in his career, with more touchdowns in his first six years (1998–2003) than any receiver in NFL history.

Moss was a tremendous offensive weapon for the Vikings and a safety outlet (and perhaps occasional crutch) for their talented quarterback, Daunte Culpepper. Moss also thrived on pressure and had his best games on *Monday Night Football,* before a national audience.

At his best Moss was one of the few true gamechangers in NFL history, so dominating he could deform an opposing team's strategy simply by being on the field. But Moss failed to realize his ultimate potential as a gamechanger. He started not running routes, ostentatiously, on plays where he was not the quarterback's target.

Moss was reviled for his poor attitude by some football commentators, but the larger issue was ignored. If Moss's only goal had been to win, he would have put the same energy into serving as a decoy as he did into catching touchdowns. This would have systemically stressed opposing defenses to the breaking point. Instead, in 2004 he pressured new Vikings coach Mike Tice to have more plays run for him. This Tice agreed to, installing his ill-fated "Randy Ratio," which gave Moss a guaranteed portion of passes thrown his way each game.

Moss was traded to Oakland in 2004, where he languishes on a terrible Raiders team. Tice was fired by the Vikings at the end of the 2005 season.

"Red Ink Rick" and "Eccentric Eddie," Chief Technology Officers

I knew "Red Ink Rick" and "Eccentric Eddie" (not their real names) during the dot-com era, and they clearly illustrate the difference between teamwreckers and eccentrics. Both are brilliant software architects, with strong personalities, and have varied and offbeat personal interests. Their abilities gave both significant influence in the Internet strategy of major companies, but they used their clout very differently.

Rick exploited his brilliance and eloquence to steer a series of Internet ventures into pursuing clever but unrealistic strategies. He used his powerful personality to manipulate other senior executives until each company ran aground. It took several ventures before investors ruefully realized that Rick's presence was inimical to profitability.

> Eddie is just as bright and innovative as Rick and (deep down) is an intellectual snob with a low tolerance for fools. But Eddie has high personal and intellectual integrity and a sense of his own strengths and weaknesses. Faced with a choice between investing all available resources into his latest brainstorm or being responsible to customers and peers, he invested in reality, to the benefit of his reputation as a reliable visionary.

SECRET 13:
Learn How to Hire and Manage Eccentrics

How can a company hire and manage talented eccentrics successfully?

Hiring Eccentrics

To hire eccentrics successfully, you must have a clear definition of the job, as well as critical success factors and qualifications, including cultural fit. Most important, you must do your research up front to make sure your eccentric is not a team-wrecker or a flake, which is an unreliable eccentric. A word of warning: If you don't have a genuine respect for eccentrics, you will have trouble distinguishing between eccentrics who are stable professionals and those who are unreliable flakes.

When hiring an eccentric, do not compromise your standards of reliability, motivation, or production. An eccentric should be all these things, albeit in an alternative fashion.

The Tampa Bay Buccaneers selected Warren Sapp in the 1995 draft despite a serious commitment to drafting high-character players. Their in-depth evaluation of Sapp before the draft gave them confidence that other teams did not have. "Whatever other issues you may have had, you knew Warren was not going to be unsuccessful," then Tampa Bay general manager Rich McKay said. "He would not allow it. Some teams weren't paying attention to those issues beforehand. So when they came up, they had to pass since they had not researched them."[10]

Managing Eccentrics

Managing eccentrics successfully is largely a function of respect. The executive must respect the individual, regardless of quirks, and earn the eccentric's respect as a manager, for competence, consistency, and defending the eccentric from external distractions. Being an eccentric executive doesn't hurt, but I have known many linear, left-brained executives who were greatly respected by talented, eccentric subordinates.

Bottom line, if you hire the right people, set a clear direction for the organization, and are a competent manager, you can manage talented individuals differently, as long as they are committed to leveraging their abilities toward the goals of the organization. But it is pointless to ask someone to stop being unusual on command; it is like asking a terrier not to dig in the backyard.

Whether you are managing others in sports or business, remember that *competent* is not a dirty word. Encourage eccentrics to bolster their weaknesses. It is unlikely they will become great at tasks they don't do well now or they dislike doing. But their achieving competency will allow you to rely on their strengths without having to supervise them closely.

HIGHLIGHTS

The frustration of managing difficult personalities, in sports or business, often leads to fantasies of winning with a team of hard workers with above-average talent and being able to avoid quirky personalities altogether. The danger in this is achieving consistent mediocrity.

SECRET 10
Seek talented eccentrics

SECRET 11
Distinguish eccentrics from teamwreckers

SECRET 12
Recognize the varieties of eccentrics

SECRET 13
Learn how to hire and manage eccentrics

CHAPTER 4

4TH AND INCHES

Recognize That Ability Is Hard to Measure

You have to be able to tell the difference between forty speed and play speed . . . a 4.6 guy who [is] a good athlete, has balance, body control . . . might play faster than a guy that runs a 4.5 or 4.55.

—Boyd Dowler, Atlanta Falcons scout[11]

The rigorous quantitative assessment of personnel is ubiquitous in both the NFL and business today. Nevertheless, in both settings there are bargains to be had on potential stars who do not fit the quantitative mold yet succeed at everything they do.

The systematic quantitative assessment of potential hires began in World War II, the first conflict requiring numerous complex, knowledge-based, roles for troops. The U.S. armed forces segmented draftees using the Army General Classification Test

(AGCT), based on the tools of intelligence testing developed in the first decades of the twentieth century.

The NFL draft was an unsophisticated affair prior to the 1960s. Most teams selected players based on their college awards or the positive review of a scout or associate. But several things changed during the sixties. First, the advent of national television contracts made the NFL a big business. Soon, competition with the new American Football League (which was merged into the NFL in 1970) for star players led to million-dollar contracts. As a result, the costs of making poor selections suddenly became much higher and were spotlighted in the national media.

The NFL's talent selection process was brought into modernity by visionaries such as Tex Schramm and Gil Brandt of the Dallas Cowboys, a 1960 expansion team. They recognized that "gut-level" decisions were often no more than loose impressions, influenced by the bias of the observer. Even accomplishment in the college game was not necessarily an accurate indicator of professional performance—the professional game was much faster, and it was oriented more toward passing than running the ball.

The Cowboys' scouting and drafting innovations were the foundation of the franchise's success over the next two decades. The team developed a comprehensive set of required physical measurements for draftees and used the emerging computer systems of the 1960s to automate the collection and analysis of player data. They also extended testing and evaluation to prospects from smaller schools, particularly traditionally black colleges, which had previously been largely ignored by professional teams.

SECRET 14
Choose Playing Speed over Track Speed

The Football Hall of Fame is filled with players who lacked world-class speed but whose playing speed made them far more successful than sprinters who were not football-savvy. "Playing speed" in football is a combination of awareness and body control. What distinguishes each quality?

Awareness

Awareness is what allows New England's Tom Brady, a quarterback of only average speed, to have the uncanny ability to step away when a defender is about to pull him down from behind. This gives him the functional speed of a much faster player in avoiding sacks.

Wayne Gretsky and Magic Johnson are stars from other sports who had average speed but saw the game in slow motion, which allowed them to step around opponents seemingly frozen in place.

Body Control

Control involves flexibility, particularly joint flexibility; balance; and the ability to start and stop quickly and to move quickly at sharp angles. Football scouting reports consistently focus on a player's hips.

Loose hips are critical for cornerbacks, who must mirror the moves of receivers attempting to spring free, and offensive linemen, who must sink into a powerful low stance to block defenders rushing the quarterback. A fast but stiff-hipped cornerback will quickly lose track of a slower wide receiver running his route and making sudden changes in direction.

> ### *Jerry Rice's Secret—It's in the Hips*
>
> Jerry Rice is considered the greatest wide receiver in the history of the NFL, though he had good, not great, speed. But watching films of him running routes during off-season training is a revelation. He made his cuts from the hips, so sharply and quickly that he momentarily disappeared in plain view, like a Ninja assassin. Others might beat him in a sprint, but in a football game he could spring free at will.

In business, too, events rarely move in a straight line for long. There are unforeseen hurdles and unexpected changes in markets—the difference between real life and theory. Some individuals are resilient and relentless in the face of change. They are only talented, not gifted, but they do not slow down under pressure. Others have a lower tolerance for ambiguity and become rigid and discouraged under difficult conditions, despite their elite abilities.

Speed is a powerful advantage to winning, in football or business. Still, there are many ways to be unproductive and lose. Being slow may be one; but, so is running the wrong way, running in circles, or choosing not to finish the race.

 ## SECRET 15
Don't Confuse the Map with the Territory

Metrics of ability are critical in football and in the workplace. But as mathematician Alfred Korzybski said, "The map is not the territory." However useful quantitative models and statistics are, they are still abstract representations of reality. Mindless adherence to statistical averages results in the selection of average performers.

Every year, there is at least one prospect in the NFL draft whose scouting report says something like, "He'd be a first round pick if he were two inches taller." Often that player was a three-year starter, an All-American, and a team leader. He is strong, fast, smart, and physical and he has excelled at every level. The player is drafted in the second or third round, and he quickly becomes a Pro-Bowler and the heart of his team, despite those two missing inches. Table 6 presents three recent examples of this phenomenon.

TABLE 6 *Underestimated All-Americans, Future Pro-Bowlers*

Player, Position, Team	College Accomplishments	Perceived Limitations	NFL Success
Nathan Vasher, cornerback, Chicago Bears (drafted 4th round, 2004)	3-year starter for Texas Longhorns; school record 17 interceptions; All-American punt returner	Ordinary (4.48) time in 40-yard dash; lean frame	Led Bears with 5 interceptions in rookie season; voted to 2005 Pro Bowl
Lofa Tatupu, inside linebacker, Seattle Seahawks (drafted 2nd round, 2005)	All-American defensive leader of USC national champions in 2003 and 2004; physical, brilliant signal caller, enormously productive	At 5'11", 226 pounds, considered too short to be a classic linebacker	Led Seahawks to Super Bowl in his rookie season; voted to 2006 Pro Bowl
Bob Sanders, strong safety, Indianapolis Colts (drafted 2nd round, 2004)	Leader of Iowa's defense; elite speed, power, and leaping ability; considered one of college football's hardest hitters and best athletes	At 5'8", considered too short to be a sure thing in the NFL	Voted to 2005 Pro Bowl, now one of the top five safeties in the NFL

In corporate hiring, rigid grade standards or degree requirements are an implicit statement that you don't trust individual hiring managers to recognize talent or to keep their standards consistently high.

SECRET 16
Reject Irrelevant Metrics

Some metrics are not only nonessential but also deeply irrelevant. For the NFL draft, players are measured on how many times they can bench-press 225 pounds, a measure that has little to do with any particular football skill. A player's time in the forty-yard dash is the most publicized of all pre-draft statistics, despite the fact that linemen rarely run farther than ten yards on any one play.

Companies that are used to "managing by the numbers" occasionally overreach in setting quantitative standards in the hiring process. Here are a couple of egregious ones.

School Daze

Companies sometimes rely too heavily on academic records as an indicator of success in the workplace, especially for experienced hires. I once encountered a company that asked candidates how they scored on their SAT college entrance exams. The fallacy is obvious—SATs are predictors of future success in college. Evaluating college graduates on their SAT scores is like checking the temperature ouside by reading the meteorologist's extended forecast in a week-old newspaper, rather than simply looking at the thermometer on your porch.

At another company, the hiring manager for a vice president of engineering role, himself a former academic, quizzed candidates on which math classes they had taken twenty years earlier.

The One-Page Résumé

Rejecting candidates based on the length of their résumé is the ultimate frivolous metric, an indicator that you lack an objective basis on which to screen résumés. Of course, résumés should be appropriate in length to the experience of the candidate, but not rigidly so.

 ## SECRET 17
Always Consider Performance Measures in Context

In major league baseball, the biggest revolution has been applying comprehensive statistical analysis to assessing player performance, as described in Michael Lewis's best-selling *Moneyball.*[12] As Dan Ackman wrote in a 2003 *Forbes* review:

> Many in baseball focus only on traditional statistics such as batting average and runs batted in. But [Oakland GM Billy] Beane . . . understands that on-base percentage (including walks) and total bases are far more determinative of a team's success than the traditional measures. . . . These insights have dramatic implications for how amateur players are drafted, who is promoted to the majors and in the trading and signing of veteran players.[13]

However useful the Moneyball approach is in baseball for identifying talent, it is fundamentally irrelevant in football, as well as in business. In baseball, each player performs individually. True, a pitcher will lose more games on a team that scores fewer runs, but his earned run average (ERA) will objectively indicate his ability.

Part of the reason baseball has such elaborate statistics is that it is easier to measure nearly every aspect of play. Each play has relatively few variables—one player pitches the ball, one player hits the ball, and one player catches the ball. In this respect, baseball resembles manufacturing, where statistical process optimization is used to measure and improve every process.

Football, on the other hand, has so many variables on each play that it resembles software development, where it is much more difficult to apply statistical process optimization. In contrast with baseball, many football positions have no obvious metrics. Here are some examples.

Offensive Line

There are no useful metrics by which nonexperts can assess an offensive line, aside from the overall production of the offense. Only a handful of expert analysts collect meaningful statistics about line play, and they do it by painstakingly reviewing film, over and over.

Defense

There are several prominent defensive statistics, such as quarterback sacks, tackles, and interceptions, but they are deceptively inadequate in judging individual play.

Sacks. Defensive ends are most likely to sack the quarterback, but their access to the quarterback is heavily dependent on the ability of the interior defensive linemen to shatter the opposing offensive line.

Tackles. Brian Urlacher, the star middle linebacker of the Chicago Bears, is renowned for his frequent tackles all over the field. But his mobility is enabled by interior defensive linemen who play in front of him and prevent opposing blockers from obstructing Urlacher's movement. In years when the Bears had mediocre defensive linemen, Urlacher's effectiveness was noticeably diminished.

Interceptions. A high number of pass interceptions is generally not an indication that a cornerback is a great defender, but that he is considered vulnerable and therefore is being targeted by the opposing offense.

Even the explicit metrics of skill positions, like the ones used in fantasy football leagues, are contextual. A good running back playing behind a great offensive line will collect gaudy statistics. Since 1998, under head coach Mike Shanahan, the Denver Broncos have had five players rush for over 1,000 yards—Terrell Davis, Olandis Gary, Mike Anderson, Clinton Portis, and Reuben Droughns—most of them mid- to low-round draft choices. The critical success factor in the Broncos' running game is their offensive line, both its personnel and its system, which emphasizes mobility, pattern blocking, and consistency of personnel.

Managing human capital with the rigor of baseball's Moneyball approach is simply not yet viable. Optimizing widgets is much easier than optimizing people, as past attempts to apply statistical process optimization to improve soft disciplines such as education or psychotherapy have demonstrated.

The field of accounting serves as a model for human capital metrics. Accounting is a remarkably sophisticated discipline, which takes into account the difficulty of accurately assessing a complex, organic entity. It acknowledges a reality that philosophers have grappled with for millennia: it is impractical, if not impossible, for humans to possess truly complete, truly current knowledge of dynamic living entities.

HIGHLIGHTS

The rigorous quantitative assessment of personnel is ubiquitous in both the NFL and business today. Nevertheless, in both settings there are bargains to be had on potential stars who do not fit the quantitative mold yet succeed at everything they do.

SECRET 14
Choose playing speed over track speed

SECRET 15
Don't confuse the map with the territory

SECRET 16
Reject irrelevant metrics

SECRET 17
Always consider performance measures in context

CHAPTER 5

MIDDLE LINEBACKER MENTALITY

Accept That You Can't Teach Desire

If you don't invest very much, then defeat doesn't hurt very much and winning is not very exciting.

—Dick Vermeil, former NFL head coach

Desire. Heart. Relentlessness. Call it what you want, but it is difficult, inefficient, and tiring to attempt to instill it in adults. As motivational author Jim Rohn has written, "Don't waste your time trying to change ducks into eagles." Hiring motivated individuals is easier than trying to instill ambition in the unmotivated.

Obviously, elite talent and motivation are preferable, in the NFL and in business. But many individuals with superior ability do not have the deep-seated motivation to utilize those talents, for a variety of root causes. They may fit into one of these two categories:

- **Not willing to pay the price.** Some never learned how to delay gratification toward a long-term goal.

- **Don't know how to pay the price.** Randall Cunningham, the talented quarterback of the Philadelphia Eagles in the 1980s and '90s, did not reach his full potential until late in his career. He ascribed his change in attitude to an encounter with Michael Jordan. Exposed to Jordan's fiery competitive spirit over a casual round of golf, Cunningham realized he had been settling for just trying to be "the best he could be," while Michael was trying to be better than everyone else.

 **SECRET 18**

Select Good Talent with Great Will over Unmotivated Great Talent

This concept can be represented visually as an equation:

(Good Talent × High Motivation) > (Great Talent × Low Motivation)

College football players who aren't self-motivated are not likely to develop that trait as professionals. Conversely, players with the inner drive to succeed are likely to do just that.

The corporate comparison here is virtually a cliché, but no less critical for being so. The business world is full of wildly successful individuals whose talent seems run of the mill.

A mid-level manager at an industry-leading technology start-up once complained to me that her company's CEO had an unimpressive track record. How did he come to run such an important company? "Easy," I responded wryly, "he founded the firm." His willingness to take risks in the face of uncertainty was more important than the limitations that might have hindered his rising in a conventional corporate setting.

Tampa Bay's Draft Strategy

[In the 1990s] the Tampa Bay Buccaneers . . . developed an uncanny knack for discovering guys who were the complete package, even in cases where other teams saw weaknesses. Where some teams focused on a lack of size and speed, the [Bucs] noticed leadership and drive. Where other teams noticed a lack of raw football talent, they recognized extra doses of heart and hustle.

• In 1993, the Buccaneers [drafted] a safety from Stanford University who was slow, undersized, and playing baseball in the Florida Marlins organization. Ten years later, John Lynch left the Bucs with Hall of Fame credentials and a reputation as one of the game's hardest hitters and one of the its most civic-minded players off the field.

• In 1995, Tampa Bay used the second of its first-round picks on Derrick Brooks, a promising, if undersized linebacker from Florida State. Brooks, like Lynch, became a perennial Pro Bowler and Hall of Fame candidate.

• In 1997, the Bucs risked the twelfth overall pick on Warrick Dunn, a five-nine Florida State running back who many teams thought was too small to be anything more than a third-down back in the NFL. [The Bucs] viewed Dunn differently, believing he possessed unusual confidence and determination. Dunn, like Brooks, became a Pro Bowl player and one of the league's most charity-minded players.

—Pete Williams,
The Draft: A Year Inside the NFL's Search for Talent[14]

SECRET 19
Look for Resilience to Prevent Burnout

Failure, in football or business, instills character in some, bitterness in others, and burnout in the exhausted.

In the NFL, burnout takes a variety of forms. A star rookie quarterback on a bad team with a weak offensive line can be sacked so often that his judgment and instincts are warped before he has had a chance to acclimate to the increased speed of the professional game. Such players may recover later in their career and play well, like Jim Plunkett did in winning for the Oakland Raiders, or they may never recover.

Some players with unique size and skills may never have particularly wanted to play at all. A lineman with unusual size and strength may have been pushed to play from high school on by coaches, parents, and peers. If they are talented enough, they can reach the professional level despite their lukewarm feelings about the game and an unwillingness to exert themselves for a goal they never truly committed to.

In a corporate setting, a hiring manager can be caught in the paradox of seeking a key employee with a proven track record yet who still has something to prove. Often it's a talented individual who has succeeded in the past but has recently tried and failed at a major venture. The lessons of that failure can be invaluable to the hiring company.

What qualities define the resilient executive who has been toughened, rather than scarred, by his "adventures"?

- **Perspective.** Gratitude, humor, and playfulness are powerful elements of durability.

- **Integrity.** Intellectual integrity is essential in order to learn from experience, and emotional self-knowledge is critical to recovery from a draining failure.

■ **Willingness to pay the price.** Many people think they are entrepreneurs, just as many think they could write a novel. The real test is doing it, even in the face of increased odds. As the saying goes, "Do or do not; there is no try."

Another challenge to a hiring manager is hiring key contributors in a maturing industry. Often, many successful candidates were successful when the industry was in a growth phase but are exhausted from the diminishing returns on their efforts that previously paid off handsomely. The software industry, for example, is a radically different business today than it was in the golden age of software of the 1980s and '90s. In the twenty-first-century Internet era, customers are focused on buying business services enabled through information technology, rather than packaged software. The technology itself is increasingly a commodity, a long-term trend.

Software is no longer a growth industry in which a great technology can be turned into a billion-dollar company by a first-rate team. Rather, it has stratified into two tiers: the successful giants such as Microsoft, Oracle, SAP, and IBM; and the niche players, who fill narrow business needs successfully and dream of (and occasionally realize) being acquired by one of the giants. IPOs, in the current economy, are not a realistic option for these companies.

Some executives are motivated by this paradigm shift, while others have not moved past the emotional exhaustion of a down market and have their tail between their legs. Avoid hiring an executive because of his or her past success in past liquidity events in your industry without examining the fit of their skill set with today's marketplace.

SECRET 20
Create an Aggressive Culture

Trying to turn ducks into eagles is futile, but you can perpetuate an eagle culture. The best football teams and corporations do.

Part of the success of the current New England Patriots dynasty is due to an organizational culture that intertwines intelligence, hard work, and aggressiveness. Head coach Bill Belichick is careful to distinguish between *swagger* and *urgency* as a critical factor for winning a Super Bowl with an overachieving team: "We didn't have a swagger last year . . . what we had was a sense of urgency, a sense of urgency about playing well, being smart, and capitalizing on every opportunity and situation that came our way."[15]

In a corporate setting, strategic alignment and operational excellence are the foundation of success, but a culture that perpetuates urgency is critical for finishing the job. In *Good to Great*, Jim Collins describes the value of establishing such a culture at Nucor, a successful steel manufacturer he studied: "The Nucor system did not aim to turn lazy workers into hard workers, but to create an environment where hardworking people would thrive and lazy workers would either jump or get thrown right off the bus."[16]

An aggressive, urgent culture is critical to successfully pursue a lean initiative like Six Sigma. Conversely, a company with a passive or change-resistant culture is likely to transmute a lean initiative into an additional layer of bureaucracy.

General Electric's success with Six Sigma contrasts starkly with the lack of impact that various lean methodologies had at AT&T. This was not due to a head start on the part of GE. In the post–World War II period, both were mass producers, rather than lean. But in the late 1990s, Jack Welch deliberately chose

Six Sigma as a weapon to make GE more nimble in serving customers. In contrast, AT&T remained a reactive organization, resistant to a culture of raw aggressiveness. Though a world-class innovator and service provider, its culture was formed by a hundred-year heritage as a monopoly, which introduced new products at its leisure.

Aggressive process also has value as a strategic weapon. Microsoft, Wal-Mart, and Dell, for example, all dominate their industries through organizational self-discipline, flexibility, and aggressiveness.

Is "aggressive lean" immoral? Not if one accepts the benefit of "creative destruction" as a key mechanism of wealth creation in a capitalist economy.

Genghis Khan's Lean, Mean Organization

Improbably, the supreme historical case of an aggressive, lean organization predates the Industrial Revolution by six hundred years.

Nearly eight hundred years after his death, Genghis Khan is widely considered the greatest conqueror in history. Between 1206 and 1258 A.D., Khan and his immediate descendants conquered nearly all of Asia and much of central Europe. Only the death of Genghis Khan's son, Ogadai, in 1241 kept the Mongolian armies from devastating the rest of Europe.

The Mongols are a fascinating organizational case study. How did nomadic tribes from a desert at the top of the world create the largest empire in history? The societies they conquered, including China and several major Muslim empires, were far larger and seemingly more sophisticated than the Mongols.

Genghis Khan can be thought of as the first lean executive, for he aggressively intertwined people, process, and technology in both strategy and execution. Uneducated and illiterate, he organized his armies to optimize efficiency and flexibility.

Structurally, the Mongols had many of the attributes twenty-first-century companies strive for. They were disciplined, yet flexible; communicated decisions accurately in real time; and efficiently used resources in a variety of innovative ways. The combination of organizational self-discipline, flexibility, and aggressiveness allowed the Mongols to defeat larger armies of that era that were rigidly organized and whose discipline was superficial.

The Mongols cultivated these efficient, collaborative qualities in their horsemen from an early age with their traditional hunts on the Mongolian steppes, where they would encircle large numbers of animals and gradually herd them together for butchering, rather than chase them down individually.

Clearly, Genghis Khan is not a moral role model. He deliberately and brutally devastated most everyone in his path. He was more interested in acquiring trading routes and technology rather than subjects, and his hordes routinely killed the entire populations of cities that resisted them. Yet there are striking parallels between the management secrets of Genghis Khan and some of the most successful modern corporations. For example, General Electric's use of Six Sigma process improvement as an aggressive weapon for change bears a benign resemblance to the Mongols' highly organized, flexible, and ruthless organization.

SECRET 21
Hire People Who Share Your Goal

It is reasonable to assume that a talented individual will choose to leverage his special talents, but it isn't necessarily so.

Consider the case of Joe Don Looney. In the 1960s, Looney's name was a byword for squandered ability and eccentricity. An incredibly athletic running back, he was considered the "Mickey Mantle of football" for his unique combination of speed and power. Looney played for three colleges before being drafted by the New York Giants in the first round of the 1964 draft. The Giants traded him after a mere twenty-five days with the team.

In *Paper Lion,* George Plimpton describes Looney's estrangement from convention:

> [When Looney] came to Detroit and began cutting practice, the Detroit coaches, who were unable to impress him, sent (future Hall of Fame linebacker) Joe Schmidt around to talk to him. Schmidt found him sitting cross-legged on the bed in his room, a big Indian blanket pulled over him, and his high fidelity equipment turned up full volume.
>
> Schmidt turned the music down, Looney watching him from the hood of his blanket, his eyes flickering. "Joe Don," began Schmidt easily, "a football player has certain responsibilities. Practice is one of them. You'd have no kind of team if the players didn't report for practice. You can see that. I haven't missed or been late for a practice in thirteen years."
>
> "Thirteen years!" exclaimed Looney. Schmidt supposed he was beginning to make an impression. "Man, you need a break," Looney went on. "You'd better take an afternoon off. Take my word for it."[17]

Five teams gave Looney a chance over a six-year NFL career, in which he accomplished nothing. He served in combat in Vietnam, joined a Hindu cult, and died in a motorcycle accident in 1988 at age 45.[18]

More recently, many were shocked when star running backs Ricky Williams and Ontario Smith were suspended after frequently testing positive for marijuana. Why would accomplished stars sacrifice their career and millions of dollars for a toke? But Williams and Smith are not crazy or stupid; Williams in particular seems bright and thoughtful. Their actions make sense if you understand their assumptions.

Tom Brady asks himself, "What would Joe Montana do?" Ray Lewis asks himself, "What would Mike Singletary do?" Ricky Williams and Onterrio Smith answer to a different muse: "What would Cheech and Chong do?" Cheech and Chong, it is reasonable to assume, would not allow "the Man" to keep them from lighting up.

Corporations sometimes hire previously successful consultants, who are presumed to share the company's goals. But often they don't. The specialists are often dedicated to their craft, rather than the overall business, or to their personal P&L, rather than the company's performance.

A *Fortune* 500 retailer of my acquaintance hired large numbers of management consultants into executive roles several years ago, in an attempt to enhance the caliber of its management team. Some were successful, but many were ineffective as corporate regulars. The problem, one of their peers (not a consultant) told me, was not one of ability or ambition, but their habit of instinctively building miniature consulting practices in whatever function they were placed. They had been rewarded in their past roles for putting consultants out on projects, not running actual businesses.

HIGHLIGHTS

Desire. Heart. Relentlessness. Call it what you want, but it is difficult, inefficient, and tiring to attempt to instill it in adults. As motivational author Jim Rohn has written, "Don't waste your time trying to change ducks into eagles." Hiring motivated individuals is easier than trying to instill ambition in the unmotivated.

SECRET 18
Select good talent with great will over unmotivated great talent

SECRET 19
Look for resilience to prevent burnout

SECRET 20
Create an aggressive culture

SECRET 21
Hire people who share your goal

CHAPTER 6

EXPENSIVE BENCHWARMER

Pay for Production, Not Potential

Guys, don't worry about the horse being blind, just load up the wagon.

—John Madden, sports commentator and former NFL head coach

A gamechanger is not someone who *can* change a game; he or she is someone who *does* change games, regularly. Beware choosing mediocre performers with high potential over individuals with seemingly ordinary ability who consistently excel.

 **SECRET 22**
Be Realistic About Potential

The Tampa Bay Buccaneers are a team that successfully changed its drafting philosophy and productivity. In Pete Williams's *The*

Draft, current Atlanta Falcons GM Rich McKay speaks about how he viewed the limits of potential when he was managing the Buc's organization: "There was too much emphasis put on potential, and not on production," McKay said. "When the word character was used, it was really talking about "characters," not character. And so we said we're going to change the way we approach this and go with overachievers. The idea was that, even if we miss on that player and they may not be Pro Bowlers, they're still going to be good players."[19]

Potential is a word that brims with hope but has vastly different meanings depending on the context and tense:

■ **Future potential.** "Possessing the capacity for growth or development."[20] This is the good sort of potential, the "what you are going to be when you grow up" variety. Even so, it is still a projection.

■ **Present potential.** "Capable of being but not yet in existence."[21] This is bittersweet potential. You are grown and possess the requisite abilities, but have yet to consistently utilize them successfully.

■ **Past potential.** This, of course, is entirely bitter. As Quaker poet John Greenleaf Whittier wrote: "For of all sad words of tongue or pen, the saddest are these: 'It might have been!'"

Present potential is the most alluring. It is the essence of any turnaround opportunity; fully developed resources waiting to be utilized more effectively. But getting underachievers to realize their full potential is a long shot. The most likely reason for their unimpressive performance up until now is their inability to self-motivate, and this is most difficult for anyone else to change.

SECRET 23
Instill the Habit of Dominating

Domination is fundamentally a state of mind, a self-fulfilling combination of ruthlessness and consistency. Growing players or executives by giving them challenging yet viable tasks is a subtle art.

There is tremendous comfort in selecting a player who has dominated at every level. An elite talent who has dominated in high school and college will by habit dominate at the professional level. Putting players of great ability in a position where they cannot quickly dominate can lower their expectations and goals, transmuting stars into role players. The NBA has learned this the hard way in the past decade.

Where Have All the Centers Gone?

The National Basketball Association's current talent base is rich, with young stars like Lebron James and Dwyane Wade and an infusion of talent from around the globe. Yet for the first time in forty-five years, the NBA is virtually bereft of great centers who can control the game on offense and defense. The legends of the past—Bill Russell, Wilt, Kareem, Moses Malone, David Robinson, and a dozen other dominating centers—are matched today only by an aging Shaquille O'Neal and an inconsistent Yao Ming.

Where have all the centers gone? In contrast to the NFL, NBA teams over the past decade came to value potential over production. Accomplished senior All-Americans like Josh Howard of the Dallas Mavericks or Jameer Nelson of the Orlando Magic were drafted at the end of the first round, long after an array of talented but undeveloped high school players had been selected.

The logic, sometimes stated explicitly, was dizzying: If potential is everything, these college seniors had already realized most of theirs. Though their accomplishments, team play, and basketball IQ were stellar, their physical ability was only above average, not Jordanesque. In contrast, the high schoolers were pure potential, allowing teams to project, or fantasize, that their selection might be the next Jordan. These prep selections were wondrously talented, and several have become NBA All-Stars. But most have underachieved, though their potential keeps them in the league for a number of years.

It is the center position that has suffered the most from the overemphasis on potential. When the top high school centers enter the NBA as skinny eighteen-year-olds, they can no longer easily dominate; they transform into teenagers being pushed around by men ten years older. By skipping the intermediate developmental stage of college play, they lose the mental habit and confidence of consistent dominance that great centers require.

NFL teams value the principle of dominating at every level much more than their NBA counterparts. In fact, NFL rules prohibit a player from entering the draft less than three years after graduating high school. As described below, dominating at every level of play has several benefits.

Proving Consistency

Even future potential is of questionable value if it is not being fully realized in its current environment. Is the prospect someone who exerts himself under all circumstances, or sporadically? If sporadically, does your organizational culture have the necessary elements that will bring out his best?

As Chicago Bears GM Tim Ruskell said in Pete Williams's *The Draft*, "Do you want the guy that has the ability but isn't going to reach that potential? No, because you don't know what you're going to get from day to day. If he's feeling good, he'll give it his all. But if he's not, then you're not going to get that premium player."[22]

Validating Potential

Are they good, or just lucky? If you are extrapolating off a single job, there is no way to know.

A marketing vice president at a new product division of a *Fortune* 500 company told me that he and his peers would sometimes spend hours debating whether a candidate's success in a previous role signified that he or she could excel in their organization. His manager would often play devil's advocate by suggesting the individual had simply been lucky, in the right place at the right time.

I suggested to him that the root cause of their dilemma was not negativity on the part of his manager, but sophistication. A single event does not constitute a statistical sample. The debates over what the candidate's single major success indicated were guesswork, to compensate for the lack of enough data points to properly analyze under what conditions the individual was likely to be successful.

The corporate equivalent of "dominating at every level" is an individual consistently having a significant, positive impact in nearly every job he has had. Don't expect to see success in every role; even superstars lose games sometimes. But if they have not dominated consistently, they are either sporadic performers or lacking in their ability to evaluate roles and choose the right employer, a shortcoming in judgment that may also manifest itself once they are on the job.

SECRET 24
Beware Workout Warriors

Each year, the NFL hosts a draft combine in Indianapolis, where the top several hundred prospects are evaluated by all thirty-two teams. "Workout warriors" are prospects whose outstanding physical abilities, when measured at the combine, lead them to be selected high in the draft, despite ordinary production during their college careers. Unfortunately, most workout warriors continue to underachieve in the NFL, just as they did in college.

How does this apply in the corporate realm? Some people's skill is testing well, but this is of scant value in the workplace. As Florida State University psychologist Richard Wagner says in Malcolm Gladwell's article "The Talent Myth," "'What I.Q. doesn't pick up is effectiveness at common-sense sorts of things, especially working with people. In terms of how we evaluate schooling, everything is about working by yourself. If you work with someone else, it's called cheating. Once you get out in the real world, everything you do involves working with other people.'"[23] The "empty suit" who is "all hat, no cattle" is the corporate version of the workout warrior.

SECRET 25
Remember That Superstars Are Overachievers

A strong case can be made that even the giants of a profession are overachievers. Bill Gates and Albert Einstein are overachievers, though each is associated with outsized ability and accomplishment in their field. Yet consider how much more they accomplished than peers of similar ability.

Bill Gates

Bill Gates is the richest man in the world and a visionary pioneer of the software industry. He grew up the son of a prominent Seattle attorney and attended Harvard. Accomplished, certainly, but is he an overachiever? Most definitely. Despite his high intelligence, Gates's true achievement was as a businessman, not as an engineer.

In the era before the IBM PC, when personal computers were still the domain of hobbyists ordering kits from the pages of *Popular Electronics,* Gates dropped out of Harvard with the deliberate intent of founding a software company to dominate the future personal computer market. Gates made repeated audacious gambles: challenging the prevailing ethic in the hobbyist PC community that software should be shared, not sold; sublimating his small company to IBM in providing the operating system for the IBM PC; and then challenging IBM for control of the PC industry.

There are hundreds of elite engineers in Silicon Valley who had Bill Gates's education and opportunities in the 1980s. Nearly all are accomplished professionals. Most have contributed to the triumph of one or more successful software companies and have several million dollars to show for it. Several have played key roles in major successes and are wealthy even by Valley standards. But only Gates was driven to prove himself over and over in the realm of business, rather than staying in the technology comfort zone in which he began.

Albert Einstein

We might assume that reimagining the relationship of time, space, energy, and matter would be based on mental gifts unavailable to others. We would be correct in that assumption.

But even if Einstein's brain was one in a hundred million, there were several dozen intellects of similar ability in his era. Einstein overachieved relative to those peers. Some did not have exposure to the educational opportunities required to develop their gifts, some lacked the emotional stability to utilize it, and others would not have had the fortitude to devise and develop the theory of relativity in the evening after finishing their day job, as Einstein did as a Swiss patent examiner.

SECRET 26
Winning Produces Money;
Money Doesn't Produce Wins

It is a rare high achiever in business or sports who doesn't aspire to be highly compensated, even wealthy. But money follows accomplishment; it does not cause it. Base compensation only needs to be high enough to attract the right person.

In a corporate setting, money is an external motivator that can only be "satisfised," not satisfied. "Satisfising" is a concept in decision theory, coined by cognitive psychologist Herbert Simon, to describe needs that people seek to meet adequately while balancing them against other factors in making their decision. Relative to job satisfaction and performance, money is only one factor (albeit a critical one) in how individuals assess success.

This is not idealistic or naïve posturing. Experienced salespeople, however ambitious, will instinctively make calculations as to how much they will enjoy the job, not only how much money it pays, understanding that they will underperform and earn less if miserable.

As Jim Collins writes in *Good to Great,* "We found no systemic pattern linking executive compensation to the process of going from good to great. . . . Not that executive compensation is irrelevant. You have to structure something basically rational and reasonable . . . but once you've structured something that makes basic sense, executive compensation falls away as a distinguishing variable in moving an organization from good to great."[24]

In football, the ultimate compliment is "He's a football player." In business, it is "She makes money everywhere she goes."

HIGHLIGHTS

A gamechanger is not someone who *can* change a game; he or she is someone who *does* change games, regularly. Beware choosing mediocre performers with high potential over individuals with seemingly ordinary ability who consistently excel.

SECRET 22
Be realistic about potential

SECRET 23
Instill the habit of dominating

SECRET 24
Beware workout warriors

SECRET 25
Remember that superstars are overachievers

SECRET 26
Winning produces money; money doesn't produce wins

CHAPTER 7

HAIL MARY

Don't Try to Fix All Your Problems with One Hire

The Patriots are resilient, almost spooky in a way.
—Paul Zimmerman, *Sports Illustrated* columnist

It is a deeply human temptation to compensate for systemic weaknesses by hiring a superstar. Unfortunately, this approach is most likely to perpetuate failure. To concentrate on individual selections rather than the system they are entering is ultimately to focus on individual trees rather than the forest.

 SECRET 27
Assess the Strength of Your System, Not Your Stars

Of course, a significant element of your system *is* your stars. But a star-driven human capital approach and a team-driven approach are radically different in their priorities, allocation of resources, and results.

The Patriots under coach Bill Belichick are the poster boys for channeling resources into strengthening the overall system versus investing in individual superstars. Belichick is considered the greatest coach in the NFL today after winning three Super Bowls in four years with talented but often injured teams. His skills at strategy, game film analysis, and innovative use of talent are without equal. But it wasn't always so.

In *Patriot Reign*, Michael Holley describes the Patriots prior to Belichick: "The Patriots lacked leadership and knew nothing of meritocracy. Theirs was a culture of entitlement and preferential treatment."[25]

The resilience of the Patriots dynasty is a large part of their mystique. Each of their three Super Bowls was won with key players injured and replaced by unknowns. In the 2001 season, Tom Brady replaced star quarterback Drew Bledsoe; in 2003 there were numerous injured starters on defense and the offensive line; in the 2005 Super Bowl (following the 2004 season) no-name cornerbacks Asante Samuel and Randall Gay replaced star cornerbacks Ty Law and Ty Poole.

The Patriots dynasty certainly has superstars. Tom Brady was underestimated coming out of the University of Michigan but is now recognized as this era's Joe Montana. Richard Seymour is one of the best defensive linemen, and Ty Law was an elite cornerback.

But ultimately, the Patriots were assembled as a system, not as a group of stars. Several of their best linebackers began their NFL career as undersized defensive ends; their offensive linemen were smart and tough low draft picks rather than gifted higher picks; and they won their first two Super Bowls with a committee of unknown running backs.

The Patriots emphasis on systemic strength over individual high achievers should resonate with corporate readers. The concept that a system is only as strong as its weakest link was popularized by Eli Goldratt in his business novel *The Goal,* which described a company identifying and improving the shifting bottlenecks that arise in dynamic real-world environments.

In many ways, Belichick has constructed a "lean" NFL team, integrating quantitative analysis and optimization (Belichick's famed obsession for and skill at dissecting game film) with enabling individual autonomy in a production environment (in this case the actual game), for the goal of flexibility and resilience.

In *Patriot Reign,* Michael Holley describes several attributes of Belichick that closely mirror lean management principles:[26]

■ **Kaizen (continuous improvement).**
[Belichick said:] "Now, there is not one person in this room—not one—who can't improve. And it starts with me . . . there's not going to be any toleration for 'I'm doing my job, someone else can do theirs better.'"

■ **Worker autonomy.**
[Belichick] is so relentless with study and preparation because of game day. What good is it if he sees it and no one else does? He would actually prefer that his players make their own adjustments on the sideline instead of watching the game.

■ **Leader as problem solver within disciplined framework.**
The essence of Belichick is that he is a problem solver. Since he has already clearly identified the problems, he is now here to offer solutions. The solutions are easy to follow. He tells the players he needs to see more effort, more concentration, and more discipline when it comes to doing their jobs.

In a business, avoid trying to hire superstars to compensate for weaknesses in other parts of the organization. For instance, hiring a sales guru is a worthy goal, but if marketing is feeble, business growth will continue to disappoint.

A robust business function upstream puts less systemic pressure on the function you are trying to improve, in the same way that an offensive line makes a running back's path to the end zone less hazardous. For example:

- In brand-intensive industries such as consumer packaged goods, a powerful marketing function paves the way for the sales force in the field.

- Wal-Mart's sophistication and resilience as a supply chain innovator diminishes the degree of difficulty of its marketing.

The Failure of the War for Talent

In his 2002 *New Yorker* article "The Talent Myth," Malcolm Gladwell, author of *The Tipping Point,* describes how McKinsey Consulting propagated the concept of the "War for Talent," and how Enron Corporation took it to its ludicrous extreme:

"The talent myth assumes that people make organizations smart. . . . In a way, that's understandable, because our lives are so obviously enriched by individual brilliance. Groups don't write great novels, and a committee didn't come up with the theory of relativity. But companies work by different rules. They don't just create; they execute and compete and coordinate the efforts of many different people, and the organizations that are most successful at that task are the ones where the system is the star."[27]

Companies like Enron promoted a corporate culture in which stars were encouraged to pursue their own visions of success without rigorous analysis of the projects viability and relevance to the organization. In football terms, these companies promoted a culture of wide receivers trying to score an eighty-yard touchdown on every play. But the history of profitable companies strongly suggests that the successful utilization of talent requires that individuals be self-disciplined in their commitment to an organization's goals. Microsoft, for example, is famous for hiring the best talent and requiring them to focus on the broader goals of the business.

If Belichick has become famous for creating superior linebackers out of undersized defensive ends like Mike Vrabel, Tedi Bruschi, and Tully Banta-Cain, Procter & Gamble is well known for hiring the intellectual cream of young military officers into its executive ranks, including current CEO A. G. Lafley, a Vietnam-era navy officer.

SECRET 28
Slow Down to Go Faster

Chuck Norris once advised Bruce Lee to "slow down to go faster," intimating that internal balance is more important than raw speed.[28] In football or business, a decisive, analytical understanding of human capital gives a hiring manager more latitude in being creative in hiring.

Pete Williams described this football dynamic in *The Draft:* "It didn't help that the Buccaneers were forever changing coaching staffs, shifting offensive and defensive schemes, and enduring constant roster turnover. Players drafted to fit one scheme became far less valuable, if not worthless, under a new coordinator."[29]

The concept of "fit to scheme" is a powerful one. In the Patriots' system, good players like linebackers Tedi Bruschi and Mike Vrabel have been positioned to achieve greatness based on specific things they do well. In a less cohesive system, they would be asked to do too much, and their shortcomings (such as limited speed) would be exposed.

An additional benefit of focusing on systemic strength, with some elite talents and many competent players, is that the less talented positions are no longer considered a crisis but rather an opportunity. The Patriots won their first two Super Bowls with average running backs, and then upgraded the position by trading for Cincinnati Bengals star Corey Dillon, with whom they won a third.

This aligns closely with Jim Collins's approach to "getting the right people on the bus" in *Good to Great,* in which he emphasizes "the degree of *sheer rigor* needed on people decisions in order to take a company from good to great."[30] Collins adds that good to great companies are rigorous, not ruthless: "To be ruthless means hacking and cutting, especially in difficult times, or wantonly firing people without any thoughtful consideration. To be rigorous means consistently applying exacting standards at all times and at all levels, especially in upper management."[31]

SECRET 29
Beware the Winner's Curse

The "winner's curse" is an economics term that refers to the dubious victory of those who win an auction by overbidding for an item at a price that is not justified by value. They won the auction, but they would have been better off losing, as their net worth was higher before they overpaid. The concept is described in detail in behavioral finance theorist Richard Thaler's book *The Winner's Curse.*[32]

Thaler has also coauthored with Duke University economist Cade Massey a paper describing how the winner's curse applies to the NFL: "The Loser's Curse: Overconfidence vs. Market Efficiency in the National Football League Draft."[33] The "loser's curse" does not refer to the suspicion of long-suffering fans that the franchise they root for is fated to lose (or to their language in voicing those frustrations). Rather, it is Massey and Thaler's application of the winner's curse theory to the NFL, based on their statistical analysis of every player drafted since 1988, and each player's subsequent success, or lack thereof.

The loser's curse is a dilemma faced by losing teams who are "rewarded" with the highest picks in the upcoming draft. These high picks ought to revitalize the losing teams, yet many teams continue to lose year after year, and show remarkably poor judgment in exercising their high draft picks.

Outsized pay for high draft picks assumes that the draft is a perfect science, and that each pick will be a superstar. But this is obviously far from the reality.

Massey and Thaler's statistical analysis determined that "teams did not have rational expectations regarding their ability to predict player performance . . . teams overestimate their ability to discriminate between stars and flops." Moreover, the desire to draft superstars leads teams to overvalue and overpay for picks at the top of the draft. "The market value of the first pick in the first round, for example, is roughly four times as high as the last pick in the first round, and the player selected first will command a salary nearly four times higher than the player taken 30th."[34]

Massey and Thaler are not suggesting that marginal players making the salary minimum are better bargains than high-paid stars. Rather, their research indicates that year after year, the majority of stars are selected in the first forty-three picks of the draft (the first round and top half of the second). The picks in

TABLE 7 *NFL Draft Pick Value Chart*

Round 1				Round 2			
Pick	Point Value	Pick	Point Value	Pick	Point Value	Pick	Point Value
1	3,000	17	950	33	580	49	410
2	2,600	18	900	34	560	50	400
3	2,200	19	875	35	550	51	390
4	1,800	20	850	36	540	52	380
5	1,700	21	800	37	530	53	370
6	1,600	22	780	38	520	54	360
7	1,500	23	760	39	510	55	350
8	1,400	24	740	40	500	56	340
9	1,350	25	720	41	490	57	330
10	1,300	26	700	42	480	58	320
11	1,250	27	680	43	470	59	310
12	1,200	28	660	44	460	60	300
13	1,150	29	640	45	450	61	292
14	1,100	30	620	46	440	62	284
15	1,050	31	600	47	430	63	276
16	1,000	32	590	48	420	64	270

Source: The Redzone.org (2005)[35]

the top half of the second round generate a remarkable number of Pro-Bowlers, yet are valued at a fraction of the picks at the top of the first round, as shown in the standard chart of draft pick values, Table 7. The point value of each pick is determined for the purposes of trading higher and lower draft choices equitably.

A team with the first overall pick in the draft could trade it for the top five choices in the second round, be virtually guaranteed to select at least one star, and avoid the protracted holdouts and exorbitant bonuses that usually accompany the first overall pick. The Patriots have successfully used this approach in building their team, repeatedly trading players and high picks to collect large numbers of second rounders.

Massey and Thaler explain that this approach is particularly effective in the era of the salary cap, which limits team payroll to a specific ceiling each year:

> Buying expensive players, even if they turn out to be great performers, imposes opportunity costs elsewhere on the roster. Spending $10 million on a star quarterback instead of $5 million on a journeyman implies having $5 million less to spend on offensive linemen to block or linebackers to tackle. Some of the successful franchises seem to understand these concepts, most notably the New England Patriots, but others do not.[36]

Massey and Thaler conclude by suggesting how the loser's curse may apply to companies who hire and overpay outside saviors:

> The implications of this study extend beyond the gridiron ... compare [the NFL draft] to a company looking to hire a new CEO (or an investment bank hiring an analyst, a law firm hiring an associate, etc.). Candidates from outside the

> firm will have been performing much of their job out of
> view. . . . In our judgment, there is little reason to think
> that the market for CEOs is more efficient than the market
> for football players. Perhaps innovative boards of directors
> should start looking for the next Tom Brady [a sixth-round
> draft choice in 2000] as CEO rather than Eli Manning [the
> number one overall pick in 2004].[37]

In a business setting, companies encounter the winner's curse any time they decide a single candidate is indispensable and must be acquired at any cost. The emotional temptation to overestimate the value of individual stars from outside the organization is a powerful one. But reaching for saviors only delays the critical work of confronting hard truths and making substantial, incremental improvements.

 **SECRET 30**
Recognize and Buy Value

In the value investing method made famous by Warren Buffett and his mentor Benjamin Graham, it is not enough to recognize value—one should always attempt to buy it at a discount to allow for unforeseen complications. A large margin of safety will raise the odds that your investment will be profitable. As Buffett has often said, "In the short term, the market is a popularity contest; in the long term, it is a weighing machine."

To this extent, the theme of Moneyball applies to the NFL as well—don't define value simplistically, and don't overpay for it. There are numerous opportunities to apply this philosophy for NFL teams and for businesses.

In the NFL, teams can improve their total systemic strength by overpaying only for truly unique talents, of which there are precious few. They can also focus their higher draft picks on building strengths at those mundane positions that are compensated more reasonably.

For example, if running backs and wide receivers are not critical to winning, why not draft them in later rounds, after the offensive linemen who enable their success? If great safeties take the pressure off your cornerbacks, and safeties are less expensive than cornerbacks, then they represent value. As columnist Andrew Perloff wrote in *Sports Illustrated*,

> The best teams spend big money on quarterbacks and that's about it. Free-agent acquisitions at other skill positions get fans excited but don't generally improve teams. If a team's offensive line is in bad shape, Jerry Rice . . . could line up at receiver and wouldn't catch the ball. If you look at every champion since 2000, none has had a big-impact receiver. Only two of the last six champs had a wideout with more than 1,000 yards receiving: Troy Brown (1,199 for the Pats in '01) and Keyshawn Johnson (1,088 for the Bucs in '02).[38]

For corporate hires, it is important to question if there are any talents so unique that they justify overpaying for. The answer is almost certainly no. If value is measured by the output of the organization, and overpaying key individuals ignores weaknesses that make the star's output ineffective, where is the logic in pursuing a star strategy?

HIGHLIGHTS

It is a deeply human temptation to compensate for systemic weaknesses by hiring a superstar. Unfortunately, this approach is most likely to perpetuate failure. To concentrate on individual selections rather than the system they are entering is ultimately to focus on individual trees rather than the forest.

SECRET 27
Assess the strength of your system, not your stars

SECRET 28
Slow down to go faster

SECRET 29
Beware the winner's curse

SECRET 30
Recognize and buy value

CHAPTER 8

THREE AND OUT

Don't Hire by Habit

Winning is a habit. Unfortunately, so is losing.
—Vince Lombardi, former head coach, Green Bay Packers

The NFL and the global economy are starkly egalitarian environments, where production and success are everything. Beware drafting players or selecting employees based on habit and comfort level.

 **SECRET 31**
Draft the Best Player, Not Best at Position of Need

"Draft the best athlete, not for need" is an accepted axiom of the NFL draft, though one not always heeded. Teams that have a particular personnel weakness often feel enormous temptation to select the best player available at that position. If that player is overrated or a poor fit for the team's personnel schemes, he will be selected far higher than his potential justifies, especially at high-profile positions such as quarterback, defensive end, and left tackle.

In the 2005 draft, the Buffalo Bills selected Ohio State safety Donte Whitner number eight, at least ten spots above his commonly perceived value, after the top-rated safety, Michael Huff of the University of Texas, was selected seventh by the Oakland Raiders. Whitner's rookie season suggests he will have an excellent career, but his selection so early in the draft is dubious from a "value" perspective.

Drafting to improve a key weakness is fine if the player selected is of similar ability to those available at other positions. Otherwise, select the best available athlete, even if he plays a position where you already have talented players. If an organization can find productive tasks for them in the near term, stockpiling individuals of ability and ambition can be a powerful strategy for success.

This principle of drafting for general excellence rather than specific need only applies to positions that strengthen the team systemically, as described in chapter 7. A team can't have too many great offensive linemen, or defenders at any position, but it can have too many players at one of the offensive skill positions—quarterback, wide receiver, or running back—especially if the offensive line remains mediocre.

The Detroit Lions provided a vivid lesson that you can have too much offensive star talent when they used a top ten draft pick on a wide receiver in 2003 (Carlos Rogers, #2), 2004 (Roy Williams, #8), and 2005 (Mike Williams, #10). Their offensive line remained substandard, however, and this hindered the development of the three college stars, as well as young quarterback Joey Harrington, drafted third in 2002. By 2007, only Roy Williams was developing into an NFL star. Rogers was out of the league, Mike Williams was traded to the Oakland Raiders, and Harrington was traded for a pittance to the Miami Dolphins. In the 2007 draft, Detroit selected yet another wide receiver, Calvin Johnson, with the second pick of the draft.

"Best athlete" in a business context implies a hire most broadly talented relative to his or her function—sales, marketing, operations—with the flexibility to adapt to changes in your business. In other words, hire based on ability, not narrow fit.

SECRET 32
Hire from Similar Industries, Not Necessarily Your Own

An NFL personnel trend in recent years is the rise of players from sports other than football, when the skills of that sport translate well into success at specific NFL positions.

Antonio Gates of the San Diego Chargers is the best tight end in the NFL, despite not playing college football. Gates was a college basketball player at Kent State University, a physical, athletic power forward, who at 6'4" was several inches too short to have a viable NBA career. But his size, athleticism, and basketball skills involving hand-eye coordination and using his body to "box out" and create space from defenders correlate closely with the requirements of an NFL tight end.

The most unusual example of this phenomenon is Cincinnati Bengals offensive lineman Stacy Andrews, who was an All-American track athlete at the University of Mississippi. Realizing he would be better able to monetize his 6'7", 340-pound physique in the NFL, he began playing football as a college senior, and has quickly acclimated to professional football, leveraging the power and exacting technique developed as a track star.

Companies often assume that candidates from their own industry will bring the most value. But executives from other industries can help a company leapfrog its competitors by bringing in expertise from outside. After all, the benchmarking of best practices is classically done outside one's own industry. An equation visually sums it up:

$$Ability + Craft = Transferability$$

IBM Under Lou Gerstner

Consider the example of IBM hiring Lou Gerstner as CEO in 1993. IBM's market share and profitability were eroding due to its difficulty in adjusting to the growth of PCs and UNIX workstations. IBM chose Gerstner, its first CEO from outside the company and from outside the computer industry.

Gerstner was highly successful in the role, and changed IBM's culture to that of an eclectic technology services company. IBM's market value rose from about $29 billion when he took over in 1993 to $181 billion when he gave up his CEO title in March 2002.

IBM selected Gerstner because it recognized that, above all, the company needed a strategist to determine what customers really wanted and a change agent to transform IBM's engineering-oriented culture to a customer-driven culture. In this light, Gerstner's track record as a McKinsey strategy consultant, a turnaround specialist at Nabisco, and a builder of financial services product lines at American Express made Gerstner a great fit.

An incident from early in Gerstner's tenure at IBM illustrates the value he brought to the company by not being of

the computer industry. Soon after Gerstner's hire, a maga-
zine article described his speaking to a large group of IBM
employees. An engineer in the audience asked: "How do
we reconcile internal competition across product divisions?"

The question was a powerful one. IBM was facing Clay
Christensen's "Innovator's Dilemma," attempting to balance
new and mature products. It had invented RISC workstations fifteen years before, and had built a first-rate product
in the RS-6000. But the sale of these machines often as
not cannibalized sales of the mainframe or mid-range
product groups. Politics were rampant.

Gerstner answered simply: "Whatever the customer
wants is right." At the time it seemed that Gerstner had not
understood the depth of the question and was giving a
managerial platitude in response. In retrospect, his
response showed wisdom. The end result of the trend of
distributed technology was the hardware, and ultimately
even the systems software, becoming a commodity. The
customer had a multitude of choices, none of which provided high margins to the vendor. But integrating these
pieces still represented high value and profits. Gerstner
successfully led IBM toward that goal.

SECRET 33
Beware Hometown Heroes

When choosing between two players of equal talent, do not
choose the local college star who will "sell tickets." Success in
the future, not the past, sells tickets; fans will adore a superstar
wherever he is from. After all, it was excellence that made the
college star a star in first place. For example, Joe Namath, a

Pittsburgh native, was revered by locals in Alabama and then New York based on his performance and charisma.

NFL teams rarely select a player based on local popularity, though in 2006 the Houston Texans experienced significant public pressure to select University of Texas quarterback and Rose Bowl hero Vince Young with the draft's first pick. In business, select extraordinary talent from different cultures, rather than settling for ordinary candidates who fit your cultural comfort zone. In a global economy, "success sells tickets."

Another form of "hiring hometown heroes" is how women are treated as an economic resource. In his 1998 study "Spotting the Losers," Ralph Peters (at the time a U.S. Army intelligence analyst) wrote of how the subjugation of women guaranteed failure in the global economy: "The math isn't hard. Any country or culture that suppresses half its population, excluding them from economic contribution and wasting energy keeping them out of the school and workplace, is not going to perform competitively."[39]

At the positive end of the spectrum, Peter Drucker describes in *Innovation and Entrepreneurship* how Citibank took advantage of societal changes in the 1970s to upgrade its human capital. In the mid-1970s, Citibank was seeking to grow as a global financial power by increasing the intellectual caliber and aggressiveness of its mid-level management. Concurrently, the rise of feminism led to the top MBA programs producing large numbers of women graduates.

Rather than attempt to perpetuate the traditional old-boys network commonly associated with banking, Citibank deliberately hired large numbers of these elite, ambitious young women, increasing the caliber of its workforce and making a statement of valuing performance over tradition.

 ## SECRET 34
Avoid "Cogs in the Machine"

Some college football programs are so successful that the system makes good players appear great, but they then revert to ordinary in the pros. Teams selecting Big Ten running backs or offensive linemen run this risk; many of these schools have such powerful running attacks that ordinary talents can appear dominant within the overall production of the system.

In business, companies are sometimes blinded by the halo effect of a candidate from an elite competitor. But success in a smoothly functioning system often doesn't translate into success in a turnaround effort. Certain high-profile companies, like NFL teams, develop blinding reputations. The opportunity to hire an executive who worked with an industry legend, like a coach associated with a famous football dynasty, should be examined carefully, not thoughtlessly acted on.

Often these individuals are mandarins, bureaucrats who administered an empire built by someone else. Look for these warning signs:

- **Staff, not line roles.** They will have managed very large organizations, but their track record of autonomously growing businesses will be exceptions to their staff positions. In coaching terms, they will have been the offensive coordinator to a charismatic head coach, but not a head coach in their own right for any length of time.

- **Activity, not accomplishment.** They are often the first to arrive and last to leave. Do workaholics win? Only if they are doing the right work.

■ **Jargon, not strategy.** These technocrats are often efficient strategic planners, and speak effortlessly in the industry's specialized lingo. But they are not creatively strategic themselves, or have not demonstrated the ability to execute on their ideas.

SECRET 35
Seek Large Talents at Small Schools

As described in chapter 4, one of Gil Brandt's innovations as vice president of player personnel of the Dallas Cowboys in the 1960s was methodically scouting, evaluating, and selecting prospects from smaller schools, particularly traditionally black colleges, which had previously been off the radar of pro teams. The Cowboys benefited from these selections for years before the rest of the league adapted the same practices. In the current era, the bulk of NFL players come from Division 1A football programs such as Miami and Ohio State. Yet small schools frequently yield clusters of NFL stars.

In 2006, New York's Hofstra University produced wide receiver Marques Colston, a top offensive rookie for the New Orleans Saints despite being drafted in the seventh round of the draft, and Willie Colon, an offensive lineman who appears to have a bright future with the Pittsburgh Steelers. Hofstra's previous football notoriety consisted of a Bill Cosby comedy routine from the early 1960s about Hofstra dominating Cosby's hapless Temple Owls, during his own college playing days.

Brand Name vs. Generic Schools

Elite college programs in football and academics generally earn their reputation, but often the "brand name" schools are closely matched in quality by "generic brands." Third-rate schools rarely produce stars, but second-tier schools can be goldmines of talent.

For example, there are numerous schools nationally that could be considered a "poor man's MIT"—small, high-quality engineering research schools such as the New Jersey Institute of Technology and Illinois Institute of Technology with first-rate applied engineering PhD programs and global reputations. These schools don't have the name recognition of MIT or Cal Tech, but they are highly respected in their areas of focus.

An MBA Is Not the Only Measure

Requiring MBAs for executive roles is another variant of this bad habit. Though recruiting at top MBA programs is an efficient way to find elite talent, requiring an MBA for a role is a substitute for rigorous job design and talent evaluation.

Formal credentials are valuable, as long as the bearer of them has also conquered real adversity. If he hasn't, he faces the danger of equating success with climbing an organization pyramid. But at the upper reaches of government or business, there is no longer a pyramid to climb. The challenge becomes either creating new steps or a new endeavor altogether.

HIGHLIGHTS

The NFL and the global economy are starkly egalitarian environments, where production and success are everything. Beware drafting players or selecting employees based on habit and comfort level.

SECRET 31
Draft the best player, not best at position of need

SECRET 32
Hire from similar industries, not necessarily your own

SECRET 33
Beware hometown heroes

SECRET 34
Avoid "cogs in the machine"

SECRET 35
Seek large talents at small schools

CHAPTER 9

4TH QUARTER COMEBACK

Learn to Hire Gamechangers

If you know where you stand, you can dance.
—Michael Kelly, former *Washington Post* columnist

Does your organization align the hiring process for executive roles with its business goals? Probably not—the hiring of executives and senior professionals critical to the success of new initiatives is rarely managed with the same rigor as other strategic functions.

Imagine you are the CEO of a financial services company who wants to improve the firm's ability to distinguish itself from competitors and reverse shrinking profit margins. Marketing was previously handled by the senior vice president of sales, and consisted primarily of trade shows and advertising. The CEO creates a new position of vice president of marketing and sets out to find the perfect candidate.

The position is expected to be filled in four months, which seems like plenty of time. But eight months later, the position is unfilled, even though dozens of quality candidates have been interviewed and three offers have been extended and rejected. Or in a worse scenario, a star MBA consumer marketer is hired but then let go after a year of trying to build a consumer brand, even though your firm sells only to businesses.

What happened here? Most likely, because the hiring process was not managed systematically, key questions that should have been answered earlier were left unresolved, hampering the ability to hire the right person for the job. These might include questions such as:

■ What does marketing mean to this company? Is it brand building, new product introduction, channel strategy, or all three?

■ Will the position report to the CEO or the senior vice president of sales? Will marketing be an independent function or primarily sales support?

■ Will the right candidate come from a financial services competitor, a consulting firm, or a consumer marketing giant like Procter & Gamble?

This is no longer an occasional issue for organizations. Companies in knowledge-based industries may be hiring hundreds or even thousands of managers and senior professionals who earn a total individual salary of over $100,000. The cost of these suboptimized recruiting processes for senior roles is high:

■ Opportunity cost. A six-month delay in bringing a new product to market can give competitors a critical advantage.

■ Dollars spent on hiring (i.e., on advertising and search fees)

- Wasted time of hiring executives, Human Resources, and others involved in the hiring process

- Frustrated candidates. The recruiting process is the candidates' primary window into an organization. If they perceive disorganization or confusion, they may fear it is representative of the firm's culture and decline the job should it be offered to them.

What is the root cause of complexity in executive and professional hiring?

- The procedures for hiring for executive and professional positions are often overly complicated.

- These roles often have matrixed reporting relationships, so more decision makers have input into defining the role and interviewing candidates.

- Executive and professional positions today require multiple competencies—functional competency, industry knowledge, and technological competence. This is particularly true in service industries.

This dynamic is particularly common in newly created professional roles that are at the intersection of business and technology. These knowledge-based roles frequently have matrixed reporting relationships and subtle requirements in both hard (organizational) and soft (cultural) competencies.

These searches resemble a game of Twister, with multiple constituencies and priorities represented by players' intertwining arms and legs. They eventually topple over, forcing them to begin the game over again.

Cost of Delayed Executive Hire =
(Delay ÷ Project Duration) × Net Revenue

Example: If a new product service line has anticipated revenue of $13 million over the next two years, with start-up costs of $8 million, and the general manager is hired six months late, the opportunity cost can be formulated as follows:

$$(6 \div 24) \times (\$13 \text{ million} - \$8 \text{ million}) =$$
$$(.25 \times \$5 \text{ million}) = \$1.25 \text{ million}$$

The following model for selecting gamechangers, consisting of five final secrets, is intended to guide an organization seeking to optimize the fit of a key hire to the evolving needs of the organization. Recommended participants are the hiring executive (or board member coordinating the hiring process) and the senior Human Resources executive. A facilitator is recommended to guide the process, question assumptions, and document decisions and action items.

In this model, a Human Resources or Human Capital representative can diagnose and turbocharge the recruiting process, much like a great offensive line facilitates a productive offense.

 ## SECRET 36
Highlight the Business Case

The first step toward hiring a gamechanger is to be clear about what the game is, in business as in football. From a big-picture perspective, what is the business outcome this position will be responsible for? In other words, what is the business case?

In a football context, the New England Patriots have focused on the changing landscape created by free agency and the salary cap in building their dynasty.

In *Managing in a Time of Great Change,* Peter Drucker has described the concept of a company's "theory of business," its underlying strategic assumptions about its market and its own goals. It is critical, says Drucker, that a business's "assumptions about environment, mission and core competencies must fit reality."[40]

Being able to concisely articulate the business case is vital to the efficient hiring of gamechangers. Hiring the right executive for your business requires your being able to answer the tough questions as to what has changed in your market, and what the critical factors for success are.

This information already exists within your organization—it was the basis for allocating capital to this endeavor. Reviewing the business case and summarizing the critical relevant aspects should take thirty to sixty minutes, not half a day.

This exercise assumes that the position is senior enough to have a specific deliverable relative to strategic goals, and that it is a role tasked with doing something new, or at least doing something differently.

Questions for Highlighting the Business Case

1. What is the desired outcome of the business unit or function?
2. What has changed about your market and industry?
3. Perform a gap analysis comparing the current competencies of your business with the capabilities required to achieve your future strategy. What are the critical success factors? Which competencies are currently lacking?
4. What do you *need* the person hired into this role to accomplish in his or her first eighteen months? What secondary goals would you *like* him or her to accomplish?
5. Are the goals set for this individual viable under current market, industry, and organizational conditions? Have sufficient organizational resources been allocated to support the executive in achieving these goals?

SECRET 37
Define the Organization

New positions often have an insufficiently defined or an inse-cure organizational foundation. A structure built on an unbal-anced foundation is likely to collapse under pressure.

Some NFL teams are notorious for organizational dysfunc-tion, which contributes to a losing environment. The first step in the New York Giants turnaround in the early 1980s was their

---

Questions for Defining the Organization

1. Does the executive have the scope of control necessary to achieve established goals?
2. Is the organizational structure the one you would choose if you were newly designing the organization? How is it different from the old one, and why?
3. Is the organizational structure based on benchmarked best prac-tices, or the creative opinions of key individuals? Resist the temp-tation to get overly creative in designing the scope of control of the executive role. Most businesses or functions have a short list of organizational models accepted as best practices. Choose one, and tweak it if necessary. Save your innovation for products and services.
4. Is the organizational structure substantially influenced by consid-erations of personality or politics? In the real world, they usually are to some degree. Identify them, acknowledge them, and move forward, unless they are crippling to the endeavor.
5. In a matrixed organization, does the position have clearly defined responsibilities and goals (formally and informally) versus those of peers?

hiring of George Young as general manager, who had the power to resolve arguments among the various members of the Mara family, which owned the team.

 ## SECRET 38
Specify Responsibilities and Qualifications

Never postpone *any* critical decisions about a job's responsibilities and qualifications into the interviewing process. Make a firm decision and alter it later if you need to—you'll find you rarely do. The root cause of much, if not most, inefficiency in the hiring process is due to decisions that were never decided, like a game of musical chairs in which you hover above a chair but never actually sit in it.

NFL teams that lack a firm, reality-based plan for building a championship team are unlikely to reach their goal. If their plan is only partially defined, they will be tempted to select talented players who don't fit the overall scheme.

Hiring managers often say they are 85 percent sure what the position will be responsible for, and they will use the interviewing process to figure out the last 15 percent. Or they insist that they have a broad idea of what the right person looks like, but won't know for sure until they interview candidates and get a sense of what is available.

These executives who defend their casual approach to the hiring process would never dream of applying a similarly undisciplined approach to building a new home: "I'm mostly sure what I want the house to look like; let's start building it and then decide the details last." Allowing the last 15 percent of a house's design to remain ambiguous would result in construction costs doubling, and maybe an eyesore of a house.

> ### *Questions for Specifying Responsibilities and Qualifications*
>
> 1. What are three to five key responsibilities of the role?
> 2. What is the position's key deliverable? How will it be measured?
> 3. What are the key skills candidates will need to succeed?
> 4. What must they have done successfully in the past?
> 5. What industries do you want your candidates to be from?

SECRET 39
Market the Opportunity Before Selling It

Hiring managers take for granted that they will sell their opportunity to desirable candidates, but the marketing of the position is often neglected, making the selling more difficult, or even unsuccessful.

In the NFL, free agents usually accept the highest offer. But a star who is driven to win will have qualms about joining a losing team unless he is confident his signing is part of an overall winning strategy. For example, Hall of Fame defensive lineman Reggie White would have been unlikely to sign as a free agent with the Green Bay Packers in 1992 if he had not been confident that the Packers were on the verge of a turnaround, based on the quality of their management and coaching.

> ### *Questions for Marketing the Opportunity Before Selling It*
>
> 1. Is it easy for ideal candidates to recognize the fit, or does it involve serendipity?
> 2. Can recruiters (internal or external) communicate a strategic vision of the role?

3. Can everyone in the organization who interfaces with candidates enthusiastically communicate corporate strategy?
4. Does everyone in the organization who interfaces with candidates have a consistent message regarding the position's responsibilities?
5. Have you written a marketing job description?

Marketing Job Description

A marketing job description has a different purpose from that of an internal job description. An internal job description describes the position relative to other roles in the company, or similar positions externally. It doesn't describe the strategic context, which is consistent across the organization. A marketing job description, in contrast, is tailored to sell the opportunity to potential candidates in the outside market.

Using general, nonproprietary information from Secret 36: Highlight the Business Case, a marketing job description describes the strategic story of the position and what is special about it. Use specific terms to describe the job, and spell out the context, rather than taking it for granted. Tell a thematic story with the specifics of the role embedded in it.

SECRET 40
Implement "Lean" Interviewing

People are not widgets to be optimized. But a lean mentality to recruiting, intertwining rigor and flexibility, can be applied both in football and in business.

Based on the work you have done using the first four secrets of this chapter, you are now in a position to take a sharpshooter's approach to the interviewing and hiring process.

Questions for Implementing Lean Interviewing

1. Do you, the hiring manager, have buy-in on the position profile from your own superiors? Not having it will often result in them rejecting a candidate that the hiring manager and peers have already liked.

2. Have you defined the interviewing loop ahead of time? This includes aligning calendars of executives in the interview loop and quietly defining the input each interviewer gets in the hiring decision.

3. Are you managing recruiting with the dynamic energy of a line function? Granted, hiring is technically a staff function, but it can be managed proactively.

4. Are you filtering out the noise of excess candidates? A properly managed interviewing process should rarely have more than half a dozen candidates in consideration at one time.

5. Are you checking references for "fit to scheme" as described in chapter 7? Checking references has become a rote exercise that precedes an offer; few references are likely to say anything negative. But if you position the conversation as being primarily to seek information to better manage individuals once they are hired, those providing a reference are much more likely to provide useful information. You are giving them a reason to be candid, which is helpful to the candidate.

HIGHLIGHTS

Does your organization align the hiring process for executive roles with its business goals? Probably not—the hiring of executives and senior professionals critical to the success of new initiatives is rarely managed with the same rigor as other strategic functions.

SECRET 36
Highlight the business case

SECRET 37
Define the organization

SECRET 38
Specify responsibilities and qualifications

SECRET 39
Market the opportunity before selling it

SECRET 40
Implement "lean" interviewing

THE END ZONE

Here are my forty hiring secrets of the NFL, applied to corporate hiring. These best practices can help you improve the quality of your hires and avoid costly hiring mistakes.

1 *Discover the "true must" of the position*

2 *Hire for the needs of the future, not the past*

3 *Don't ignore key secondary attributes*

4 *Choose a "4-3" or a "3-4" sales model*

5 *Keep it simple*

6 *Eliminate teamwreckers*

7 *Understand the hidden costs of teamwreckers*

8 *Assess arrogance and disruption relative to function*

9 *Don't try to fix a teamwrecker*

10 *Seek talented eccentrics*

11 *Distinguish eccentrics from teamwreckers*

12 *Recognize the varieties of eccentrics*

13 *Learn how to hire and manage eccentrics*

14 *Choose playing speed over track speed*

15 *Don't confuse the map with the territory*

16 *Reject irrelevant metrics*

17 *Always consider performance measures in context*

18 *Select good talent with great will over unmotivated great talent*

19 *Look for resilience to prevent burnout*

20 *Create an aggressive culture*

21 *Hire people who share your goal*

22 *Be realistic about potential*

23 *Instill the habit of dominating*

24 *Beware workout warriors*

25 *Remember that superstars are overachievers*

26 *Winning produces money; money doesn't produce wins*

27 *Assess the strength of your system, not your stars*

28 *Slow down to go faster*

29 *Beware the winner's curse*

30 *Recognize and buy value*

31 *Draft the best player, not best at position of need*

32 *Hire from similar industries, not necessarily your own*

33 *Beware hometown heroes*

34 *Avoid "cogs in the machine"*

35 *Seek large talents at small schools*

36 *Highlight the business case*

37 *Define the organization*

38 *Specify responsibilities and qualifications*

39 *Market the opportunity before selling it*

40 *Implement "lean" interviewing*

NOTES

1. From Pete Williams, *The Draft: A Year Inside the NFL's Search for Talent* (New York: St. Martin's Press, 2006), 209.
2. Daniel Schuker, "Summers Named Eliot Univ. Prof," *Harvard Crimson*, July 7, 2006.
3. From Williams, *Draft*, 37.
4. Robert Ringer, *Million Dollar Habits* (New York: Ballantine, 1990), 189–90.
5. Edward Yourdon, *Decline and Fall of the American Programmer* (Englewood Cliffs, NJ: Prentice Hall, 1992).
6. Robert Subby, *Lost in the Shuffle: The Co-dependent Reality* (Deerfield Beach, FL: Health Communications, 1987), 15–16.
7. From George Plimpton, *Mad Ducks and Bears* (Guilford, CT: Lyons Press, 1974), 178.
8. Williams, *Draft*, 29.
9. Tom Wolfe, "The Tinkerings of Robert Noyce: How the Sun Rose on the Silicon Valley," *Esquire*, December 1983.
10. From Williams, *Draft*, 30.
11. Ibid., 235–36.
12. Michael Lewis, *Moneyball: The Art of Winning an Unfair Game* (New York: W. W. Norton, 2003).
13. Dan Ackman, *Moneyball: The Art of Winning an Unfair Game* (book review), *Forbes,* May 28, 2003, www.forbes.com/2003/05/28/cx_da_0528bookreview.html.
14. Ibid., 19–20.
15. Michael Holley, *Patriot Reign: Bill Belichick, the Coaches, and the Players Who Built a Champion* (New York: Harper, 2004), 88.
16. James Collins, *Good to Great* (New York: HarperCollins, 2001), 5.
17. George Plimpton, *Paper Lion* (New York: Harper and Row, 1966), 70.
18. *Wikipedia.*
19. Williams, *Draft*, 27.
20. American Heritage Dictionary, Web attribution.
21. Ibid.
22. From Williams, *Draft*, 21.
23. Malcolm Gladwell, "The Talent Myth," *New Yorker,* July 22, 2002.
24. Collins, *Good to Great*, 49.

25. Holley, *Patriot Reign*, 39.

26. Ibid., 91–103.

27. Gladwell, "Talent Myth."

28. Chuck Norris, "Slow Down to Go Faster," *The Secret Power Within: Zen Solutions to Real Problems* (Boston: Little Brown and Co., 1996), 69.

29. Williams, *Draft*, 27.

30. Collins, *Good to Great*, 44.

31. Ibid., 52.

32. Richard Thaler, *The Winner's Curse: Paradoxes and Anomalies of Economic Life* (Princeton, NJ: Princeton University Press, 1994).

33. Cade Massey and Richard H. Thaler, "The Loser's Curse: Overconfidence vs. Market Efficiency in the National Football League Draft" (paper, Duke University Fuqua School of Business and University of Chicago Graduate School of Business, April 2, 2005, under review).

34. Ibid., 19.

35. Available online at theredzone.org/2005/draft/draftvaluechart.asp.

36. Massey and Thaler, *Loser's Curse*, 35.

37. Ibid., 37.

38. Available online at cnnsi.com; accessed August 28, 2006.

39. Ralph Peters, "Spotting the Losers: Seven Signs of Non-Competitive States," *Parameters* (spring 1998), http://carlisle-www.army.mil/usawc/Parameters/98spring/contents.htm.

40. Peter Drucker, *Managing in a Time of Great Change* (New York: Penguin/Putnam), 30.

INDEX